Forever Liesl

Forever Liesl

My Sound of Music Story

Charmian Carr

With Jean A.S. Strauss

W F HOWES LTD

This large print edition published in 2002 by
W F Howes Ltd
Units 6/7, Victoria Mills, Fowke Street
Rothley, Leicester LE7 7PJ

3 5 7 9 8 6 4 2

First published in the United Kingdom in 2000
by Sidgwick & Jackson

A CIP catalogue record for this book is available
from the British Library

ISBN 1 84197 532 X

Typeset by Palimpsest Book Production Limited,
Polmont, Stirlingshire
Printed and bound in Great Britain by
by Antony Rowe Ltd, Chippenham, Wilts.

For my mother,
who always wanted to write a book,
and without whom I would never
have become Liesl

Contents

PROLOGUE

My name is Charmian Carr. But many people who see me see Liesl von Trapp's face and hear Liesl's voice, not mine.

It's estimated that one billion people have seen the film *The Sound of Music*. Many of these people connect me to the character in the story and to how *The Sound of Music* makes them feel. The story of the von Trapp family is one that strikes many chords. It is a story about family and love, about loyalty and courage, about sacrifice and standing up for what you believe in.

When people look at me and see Liesl, I believe they are looking into a mirror. If the film has touched them in some way, it is because it represents the world as they want it to be. If it makes them feel love or happiness or hope, it is because they have these feelings inside them.

I am honored to have played a part in *The Sound of Music*. Being Liesl has given me many wonderful things: a family of friends who shared the experience of making the movie; the von Trapps themselves, whose warmth and spirit inspire me; and a legion of fans, worldwide, who grace me with their good wishes and lift me with their wisdom.

This is my story – but it is theirs as well.

MARIA

We stood in the hotel lobby, Nicholas and Heather and Duane and Angela and Debbie and Kym and I, awkward and uncertain. The von Trapps were easy to spot. There were six in all, the sole surviving children of Georg and Agathe and Maria von Trapp. Dressed in traditional Austrian clothes, the women in dirndls with their gray hair in braids, they stood out among the other guests.

'This is very intimidating,' Nicholas whispered into my ear. I nodded as the von Trapps glanced at us shyly, and then turned away. The seven of us who had portrayed them in the 1965 film *The Sound of Music* wanted to approach them, but this was such a momentous occasion, none of us knew how to proceed.

It was December of 1998. We were all in New York to be honored by the State of Salzburg. The von Trapps were to be awarded the Golden Decoration of Honor for the many ways in which their family had helped Austria, and we seven were to receive the Mozart Medal for our part in spreading the von Trapps' story worldwide.

In all the years since we made the film, I had never met our real-life counterparts, only their stepmother, Maria Augusta Kutschera, whom Julie Andrews portrayed in the film. In 1964, while we were filming on location, Maria traveled to Salzburg, met the cast, and was given a walk-on part. As Julie Andrews sings 'I Have Confidence' on her way from Nonnberg Abbey to the Trapp Villa, and passes beneath an arch in downtown Salzburg, in the shadows behind her is the real Maria von Trapp. Getting those few seconds on film took thirty-seven takes, between the master shot and the reverse angles, and when it was all done Maria von Trapp told director Robert Wise, 'Mr Wise, I have just abandoned a lifelong ambition to work in the movies.'

I never saw the real Maria again before she died in 1987. Now that the moment had finally arrived that I would meet the 'children' we'd portrayed, it was daunting. It felt as if we were impostors. For more than three decades, the seven of us had been applauded for being von Trapps, and suddenly we were faced with the real ones.

We all retreated to our hotel rooms surprised at how awkward that first moment felt, and wondering why we found it so hard to speak to them. I realized how much I wanted these people to accept us. We had portrayed them, but we were aware that members of the von Trapp family were not entirely enamored of the film. Since its release in 1965, they had lived with the burden of being fictionalized. Important facts about them had been changed or obscured. People expected them to be like the film characters, and were disappointed to find the von Trapps were not mirror images of the children in the film – nor did they want to be.

Unlike the story told in *The Sound of Music*, Maria, a young novice at Nonnberg Abbey in Salzburg, was sent to the von Trapp home to care not for all seven children, but for only one child. Georg von Trapp, a widowed World War I submarine captain, had contacted the abbey seeking a tutor for his twelve-year-old daughter, whose name was also Maria. The Captain's wife had died of scarlet fever, and then Maria, his third child, had been stricken by the virus. Though little Maria had survived, her heart had been weakened. She was fragile and unable to attend school.

Maria Kutschera's arrival in the von Trapp home set in motion a series of events that decades later would be the basis for *The Sound of Music*. Some parts of the story were entirely accurate. Maria, the young novice, was the latest in a long line of governesses and teachers that the Captain had hired to look after his family. He was courting an Austrian princess. And he did marry his young daughter's tutor within a year's time. But many other facts were changed.

At midday, the seven of us who'd been in the film were invited to join the vice-governor of Salzburg for lunch in the hotel's restaurant. As we were led to our table, we passed by the von Trapps sitting at their own. Once again, we all glanced at each other but no words were spoken.

Finally, the woman who was really responsible

for everything stood up at the von Trapp table. Maria von Trapp – the younger Maria, who as a frail child had been the cause of Maria Kutschera's moving into the Trapp Villa – had not only survived childhood but outlived at least four of her siblings. Now eighty-four, she strode across the room to our table. I looked into her eyes, afraid and hopeful at the same time, as she reached out her hand to me, saying, 'I felt I should come and meet you at last.'

I jumped from my seat. 'I'm so glad you did!' I gestured toward my six film siblings. 'We've all been so nervous.'

'We have, too.' She grinned. Suddenly her arms were encircling me, and my arms instantly went around her. The embrace overwhelmed me. *The Sound of Music* had affected my life in so many ways. And it all began because of this woman in my arms, with the silver braids and the face that spoke volumes of the history she has lived.

'You are beautiful,' she said to me, smiling. 'It means so much for me to meet you.'

'And I you,' I whispered.

One by one, timidly, her brothers and sisters came over to where we stood, and Nicholas and Heather and Duane and Angela and Debbie and Kym jumped up from the table to join us. The awkwardness was past, and now we were huddling close together, talking and laughing, reveling in the connection between us, as if at a family reunion – which, in a very true sense, is exactly what it was.

I hadn't expected this sensation. I hadn't expected to feel I was coming home. For the first time, I realized how much I owed this lovely woman and her family.

'This is incredible,' Maria said, reaching out to hug me again. As I held on to her, I could not help wondering about the forces that had brought us together. We were strangers, born thousands of miles apart, separated by generations and events, yet we were bound to each other, like relatives long lost. I gazed into her face and wondered what life I would have led if this robust woman had not been a sickly child. I tightened my embrace and thought back on how it all began.

A woman who lived in Wales watched The Sound of Music *307 times in the first nine months of its release. She would go to the Capitol Theater in Cardiff twice every day and once on Sunday. She would eat lunch in the cinema restaurant, see the afternoon screening, leave to have tea, then return for the evening show. After her fifty-seventh visit, the management of the theater gave her a free pass for future performances.*

Her name was Myra Franklin, and I was introduced to her in January of 1966, when I was in the British Isles on a promotional tour for Twentieth Century Fox. To be truthful, I expected her to be a bit odd. But as we chatted I realized that she was, in fact, a very nice, soft-spoken woman. Forty-seven and a widow, with a son in the RAF, she told me that the film had taught her that love is the most important thing in the world: 'love of a man for a woman, love of family, love of country.'

I smiled, nodding, but I had to ask. 'How can you watch the movie so often?'

She answered simply: 'Because it makes me feel happy.'

SOMEWHERE HE OPENS
A WINDOW

There is a flash of lightning. Liesl enters through the window. Her dress is wet and smudged with dirt. She starts to tiptoe to the hall door. Maria sees her out of the corner of her eye, but continues:

MARIA

God bless the Reverend Mother, and Sister Margaretta and everybody at Nonnberg Abbey. And now, dear God, about Liesl— (Liesl stops and gives Maria a startled look) Help her to know that I am her friend, and help her to tell me what she's been up to.

LIESL

Are you going to tell on me?

That was to be the first line I uttered as Liesl von Trapp. It was March 27, 1964, the second day of shooting *The Sound of Music* and my very first day as an actress. But on the first take director Robert Wise yelled, 'Cut!' before I even came in the window. I had missed my cue.

'Charmy? Where are you?'

Everything was choreographed: Julie's praying, the lightning, the thunder, my entrance. I was supposed to come through the window when Julie said the line, 'God bless what's-his-name.' The

15

problem was, the thunder was so loud, I could barely hear her.

'Sorry.' I had arrived on the set two hours early that day feeling tense and excited – and worried that if I didn't do well they'd just get someone else. So, when I missed my cue, I should have been concerned that my film career would be over before the lunch break. In fact, I was just too cold to care.

Minutes earlier, Bob Wise had approached me with a man who was carrying what looked like a garden sprayer. 'You know,' Bob said softly, 'in this scene you're climbing in the window after being caught in a rainstorm. Well . . . meet Mr Rainstorm.'

Without saying a word, the man lifted the sprayer's hose and doused me with water that was so cold I gasped.

'More,' said Bob as he inspected me when the man was done. 'I want to see drops beaded on her face, and her dress needs to be clinging to her body.'

The man with the sprayer adjusted his nozzle, dousing me anew. The water hit me with enough force that I staggered backward a step; it kept coming until I was totally drenched.

Then up stepped a woman who was carrying an aerosol spray can with the word 'DIRT' stenciled on it. She sprayed my dress from top to bottom with the canned dirt.

'She looks like she's been in a coal mine,' protested Betty Levin, the script supervisor.

Bob stood his ground. 'She's been climbing up a trellis in the middle of a thunderstorm, so she'd be this dirty.' He smiled. 'She's perfect.'

Filthy, soaked, and shaking, I waited to make my acting debut. The starting bell rang on the set, a red light flashed, and the film began to roll.

Not only did I miss my first cue, but I also missed my second. I shivered in the wings, awaiting my entrance, trying to keep my teeth from chattering. All I heard was Bob yell, 'Cut!' again.

I was shaking as Bob Wise approached me. For a moment I thought he was going to tell me to pack my things and head home, but he asked calmly, 'Can you hear anything back here?'

'Not really,' I said. 'Just my teeth.' I held my breath. Maybe I wouldn't get fired yet. Maybe he'd give me one more chance. And he did. Rather than make me feel like an amateur or that I was ruining the scene or upsetting his star, Bob Wise took the time to help me become an actress. His attitude always was, if there was a problem, there was a solution. 'Julie, let's have you say that one line loud. *Really* loud.'

Of course, I wasn't the only one nervous that day. Julie Andrews had far more pressure on her. *The Sound of Music* in many ways rested on her shoulders. She wasn't a superstar yet – in fact, in March of 1964, she was virtually unknown in Hollywood. Although she was a star on Broadway, Bob Wise and Saul Chaplin, the film's associate producer, had to be convinced she was photogenic

17

enough to play the role of Maria von Trapp in their movie. They were able to view some footage of her at Disney Studios in the not-yet-released film *Mary Poppins*. After seeing just a minute of Julie, in what would be an Oscar-winning performance, Bob and Saul looked at each other and said, 'Let's get out of here and hire her before someone else does!'

Still, even though they believed in Julie's potential, she was not yet a proven star in film, and had to be feeling a great deal of pressure in those first days before the cameras. She might have exploded in anger, complained that I was destroying her concentration, and demanded that they get someone a little less deaf to play Liesl. But instead she smiled at me encouragingly and knelt beside the bed to begin her prayer for the third time.

'Ready? Action!'

Julie ran through her lines. 'God bless the Captain, God bless Liesl and Friedrich, Louisa, Brigitta, Marta and little Gretl – and, oh, yes I forgot the other boy – what's his name?' I was straining to hear behind the wall of the set when all of a sudden Julie belted out, 'Well, God bless what's-his-name!'

I nearly jumped out of my skin. I slipped through the curtains of the window, and my being nervous and cold and startled all helped the scene. Liesl was *supposed* to be nervous. She didn't want to be caught; she wanted to get out of that room without Maria seeing her.

'Are you going to tell on me?' I asked anxiously.

It was my first moment ever on film, and I looked as if I knew what I was doing.

'Great!' Bob said when we'd finished. 'That was good. Very good. Let's get one more from this angle and then we'll set up for a different point of view.'

Thus began a long, cold day of filming. While I was on camera, I warmed up under the big arc lamps – and then Bob would have them douse me with water again. I began each take the same way, soaking wet and shaking. I don't know if it was Bob's intention, but it gave the scene continuity and realism.

With each successive take, acting amid all the lights and the cameras and the dozens of people began to feel natural to me. I credit Julie Andrews with making that happen. She was always supportive, always witty off camera, and always perfect when Bob yelled, 'Action!'

After many hours and fifteen different setups, we were finally done. I retreated to my dressing room and got into some warm clothes. No one came by to tell me I was fired. Before leaving the set, I checked the call sheet for the next day – and there was my name. I'd made it through my first day as an actress.

As I drove home, I thought about Julie and Bob, and how grateful I was to them. Not once did they make me feel bad about messing up those first takes. I may be the only one who remembers what happened, but even now, decades later, when

I see the film I cringe when Julie says, 'God bless what's-his-name!' Perhaps no one else notices how she emphasizes that line, but the words always jump out at me, reminding me that I missed my first cue!

That night, wrapped in a warm blanket on my mother's couch, I studied my lines for the next day. We'd be back in Maria's bedroom, shooting the song 'My Favorite Things.' The only thing that would have to be wet was my hair. Hurrah!

That was as far as I could see into my future: the next scene, my next lines, and whether or not I'd be rained upon by the man with the water sprayer. I could not possibly have imagined how being a part of *The Sound of Music* was going to change my life. Yet my future was changed forever that day in March of 1964. When I came through that window into Maria's bedroom, I passed through a portal. I left behind the child I'd been and the life I might have lived. From that moment on, I became Liesl von Trapp, and she and I would be intertwined forever.

*T*here was a man who saw **The Sound of Music** over and over at the same theater, always sitting in the same seat. Years later, when the theater was going to be demolished, he actually bought the seat.

In some ways, I don't understand that kind of obsession. I've never felt such a strong attachment to something so intangible. Yet I do understand his yearning to cling to a special memory. We all try to find ways to hold on to things that are precious to us.

The walls of my home and office are covered with photographs of the people and moments of my life that I cherish. There are mementos from my journeys that rest on my shelves, and chests full of favorite things that belonged to my children when they were younger. Perhaps I shouldn't question a man's desire to own a single theater seat in which he spent many happy hours.

In my mind, I can see this man in his home, sitting in the old theater seat. He is not a young man anymore. His hands run gently over the maroon velvet armrests – and he is smiling.

BLUE EYES

BLUE EYES

Being cast as Liesl changed the course of my life. Yet whether or not I would be selected for the role came down to something over which I had no control: the color of my eyes.

In January of 1964, Marian Garner, a friend of my mother's who was a casting agent, had exhausted her pool of young girls who looked sixteen to send to Twentieth Century Fox for a film based on the stage musical *The Sound of Music*. Marian got an anxious call from the studio. Did she know of any other actresses she could recommend? And Marian remembered that my mother had three daughters.

'Rita,' Marian asked my mother over the phone, 'can any of your girls sing and dance and pass for sixteen?'

'Charmian could,' Mom answered eagerly. 'My middle daughter. She just turned twenty-one, but she could pass for sixteen.'

I had no serious ambition to become an actress. That dream belonged to my sister Sharon, who was a year older than I was. Sharon worked hard, all the while worrying about me and my lack of resolve. 'What you going to do with your life, Charmy?' she'd ask, shaking her head. 'You walk around like a zombie. You've got to have goals, a passion!'

I'd defend myself. 'I do have goals. I want to

travel.' I dreamed of going to Europe and visiting fairy-tale castles. I was attending college part-time and working for a doctor. The doctor was an old flirt who literally chased me around his office, but I put up with him because the two dollars an hour he paid me brought me closer to a European vacation.

Mom met me at the door that night when I got home from work. 'You've got an audition for a role in a film!'

'What?'

'It's all set. You're to go to Fox Studios tomorrow and meet with the casting director.'

Mom never even asked me if I wanted to try out for the part. But I grew up in a show business family. My father was a big-band conductor and Mom had been a vaudevillian. I knew that for her my getting a part in a film would be a much bigger deal than earning a college diploma.

I had no idea that the film I was trying out for would be shot partly in Europe. In fact, Mom didn't know anything about the role. I assumed it would be a small one, since I had no professional acting experience.

With no clue as to what I was going to have to do in my audition, I drove over to Fox the next day. The secretary for casting director Mike McLean gave me a copy of a single scene. I wasn't quite sure how this worked. I glanced at the three pages, then back at the secretary, and asked in a low voice, so no one else in the room would guess how inexperienced I was, 'Do I have to memorize all this right now?'

She looked up at me. 'No, hon. You just read right from the script.'

I nodded, trying to look as if I really knew that and had just been making sure. I sat down and read through those three pages as quickly as I could. I had ten minutes to prepare before I was called into Mike McLean's office. Mike sat facing me and fed me the lines for Rolf.

> LIESL
> (lightly)
> Don't worry about Father. He's a big naval hero. He was even decorated by the Emperor.

> ROLF
> I know. I don't worry about *him*. But I do worry about his daughter.

> LIESL
> (eagerly)
> Me? Why?

> ROLF
> Well, you're . . . so . . .

> LIESL
> What?

> ROLF
> You're such a . . . baby . . .

27

(pleased – *not* frowning)
I'm sixteen. What's 'such a baby' about that?

I'd performed in dozens of shows in our basement and backyard with my sisters, and Sharon had recruited me to be in one play in college, but that was the extent of my acting experience. I read those lines as sincerely as I could, and then Mike McLean very nicely ushered me out the door. When I got home and my mother asked me how it went, I wasn't sure if I'd done a good job or not. But a few days later, Mike's secretary called me. Could I come in for a second reading?

'Yes, of course.'

'And they'll want to have you sing as well.'

'Oh.' I'd had years of dance classes but had never had a single singing lesson, so this news made me a little nervous. The only time I had sung in public was in the church choir. I expressed my concern to my mother, and she immediately sat down at our piano and told me to sing. She kept coaxing me and working with me, and by the time I went to my second audition, I was ready to sing for them.

This time I read the same scene again, not only for Mike McLean but also for associate producer Saul Chaplin. I was smitten with Saul from the first moment I met him. Tall and skinny, with a radiant smile, he reminded me of the Scarecrow in *The Wizard of Oz*. He put me immediately at ease. More than once that day, when I was nervous, I would look over at Saul and relax. It's no surprise that he ghostwrote some of the lyrics to 'I Have Confidence,' one of the two songs written specifically for the film. He always gave me confidence in myself.

Again I read the part of Liesl. I thought it a strange name and pronounced it 'Lysol.' Saul took me aside and whispered, 'It rhymes with "weasel." Lee-zil.' Then he handed me the music for the song 'Sixteen Going on Seventeen' and I sang it a capella.

The practicing with my mother paid off. I wasn't even very nervous. Saul seemed to like me very much, and I thought they were going to tell me I had the part. But again I was shown the door. I went home perplexed, sure I had failed.

Days later, I was called back once more, this time to read for Mike McLean, Saul Chaplin, and the film's director, Robert Wise. Now I was nervous. My latent ambition had risen to the surface. I wanted to be Liesl! I didn't even know how big the role was, not having seen a full script, but by then I wanted to play the part very much.

So, once again, I read and sang. Then the three of them marched me down to the dance-rehearsal stage, where choreographers Dee Dee Wood and Marc Breaux quickly showed me some of the dance steps that would ultimately be a part of Liesl's dance with Rolf in the gazebo. Now I was on my own turf. I'd been dancing since I was four years old. Finally, all those ballet lessons paid off.

The steps were not difficult for me to master, and I could tell they were all pleased. Yet, once again, they kindly led me to the door and said goodbye.

Unbeknownst to me, Robert Wise felt I wasn't right for the part the first moment he saw me: much later, I learned that he thought my eyes were too blue and would look strange on film. But two things were working in my favor.

The first was Saul Chaplin, who became my champion. 'She's Liesl,' he insisted to Bob. 'We've finally found her.'

The second was the fact that, by the time I interviewed for the part, dozens and dozens of potential Liesls had gone through the casting director's office, including young actresses named Mia Farrow, Kim Darby, Lesley Ann Warren, Teri Garr, Shelley Fabares, Patty Duke, and Geraldine Chaplin. Bob and Saul and Ernie had a very clear picture in their minds of what Liesl would be like. Their casting notes reveal the vision they had: 'She's 16 going on 17. Part child and part young woman. Sometimes fresh and snippy – but still eager and expectant, lovely – must be able to dance well.' Their notes on various other actresses trying out for the part also reveal how difficult it can be to get cast in a role. Here's what they had to say about some of the Liesl hopefuls: 'too hammy,' 'too short,' 'too tall,' 'too old,' 'too young,' *too-too!!,*' 'can't act,' 'nothing great – but nice face,' 'great looking but awful reading: too bad,' 'heavy in legs,' 'big in fanny,' 'not strong enough,' 'not outstanding,' *'not for us,' 'a little too worldly,' 'pregnant.'*

Mike McLean had seen hundreds of young actresses and Bob and Saul had interviewed several, but their Liesl still had not been found. The six other children had already been cast, as had Julie Andrews and Christopher Plummer, and they were already in rehearsal. So Bob and Saul were at a point where they *had* to find the actress for the part. Saul fought hard for me: 'Let's give her a try.'

Bob Wise finally agreed that Saul could give me a screen test to see how my eyes looked. But a soundstage wouldn't be available for my test for two weeks. Saul hired me without a contract, telling me I was temporarily Liesl and warning me that I wouldn't be permanently cast unless I passed the screen test two weeks down the road.

Despite this caveat, I was thrilled. I quit my job at the doctor's office that very afternoon and the next morning drove to the Fox lot, fresh and exuberant. Even though I only had the job conditionally, I was excited. I had a job as an actress in a movie!

Whether or not I would ultimately become Liesl, however, hinged not on how well I could sing or dance or act, but on how my blue eyes would look on film. Life is like that sometimes – determined by things you can't control, like who your new governess turns out to be, or the color of your eyes. All we can do is look straight into the lens and let fate lead us where it will.

*O*ver the years I've heard from many people who saw The Sound of Music *on their first date. Many of their stories are similar to one from a couple in Dallas.*

'It was a blind date. We met in the fall of 1965 through a mutual friend, and we went to the Belle Meade Theater in Nashville to see *The Sound of Music. We loved it: the music, the whole thing.*

'We were married exactly a year later, in September of 1966 – and *The Sound of Music* was still playing at the Belle Meade. It had been there through our entire courtship.*

'Kids nowadays might think that's not a big deal. But back then there weren't a dozen theaters in a complex. The Belle Meade was one of the few theaters in Nashville, and it had only one screen. It was unheard-of for a movie to be in a theater for so long. That film had staying power.*

'So did our blind date. We've been married for thirty-three years and have two wonderful children, both grown now. We'd have to say *The Sound of Music* was a great date movie!'*

LET'S START AT THE
VERY BEGINNING

On my first day as Liesl, I was taken to Soundstage 15 at Twentieth Century Fox and marched to the head of a line of six children. 'You stand here,' I was told.

I looked over and for the first time set eyes upon six young people ranging in age from thirteen to five. They were not yet Friedrich and Louisa and Kurt and Brigitta and Marta and Gretl. They were still only Nicky Hammond and Heather Menzies and Duane Chase and Angela Cartwright and Debbie Turner and Kymmie Karath. They had not yet been transformed into von Trapps, nor had I. But I felt something unexpected when I was placed at the head of that line. It was as if we were all instantly bonded in some special way: we were a family.

These were very serious children. They had been selected from hundreds of young actors and actresses who had auditioned, including Kurt Russell, Richard Dreyfuss, Ann Jillian, the Osmond brothers (Alan, Wayne, Merrill, and Jay), Veronica Cartwright (Angela's sister), Jon Provost (of TV's 'Lassie'), Tommy Norden ('Flipper'), and Jay North ('Dennis the Menace'). They were chosen on a number of criteria: appearance (the Osmonds' hair was too black), poise, professional credentials (Richard Dreyfuss couldn't dance), and acting ability. Bob and Saul strove to find talented young actors who looked as if they might have come from the same family. In fact, they had a wall filled with pictures of children they were auditioning, and they spent a lot of time moving the pictures around, trying different combinations, in their effort to create the film's von Trapp family.

Saul Chaplin remembered clearly the day Kym Karath came in to read for the part of Gretl. 'She marched right in with a portfolio under her arm and declared, "I'm exactly who you're looking for, I've been in three films already."' Saul turned to Bob Wise and whispered, 'Get her out of here before she's climbing the walls.'

But Bob told him Kym *was* exactly right for the role. 'You want a child who's confident, who wants to perform for you. She's perfect.'

Over the next months, I would learn how special each child was, but that first moment I met them, what struck me was how beautiful they were as a group. They already looked like a family. I had some catching up to do. They had been in rehearsal for several days. And though they didn't tell me about it that day, they later revealed to me that I was not the first Liesl.

'They kept trying different ones out on us,' said Nicholas (Friedrich). 'I don't remember any of their names. But there were four or five other Liesls before you arrived.'

'They'd come in for a rehearsal or two,' said Heather (Louisa), 'and then they'd be gone.'

'I just remember we were glad when you arrived,' Angela (Brigitta) said. 'Of course, we thought you were permanent. We didn't know you weren't under contract. We didn't know you were in limbo.'

I did feel strange those first days, as if I were a foster child visiting a family, desperately wanting to belong, but not sure if I was going to be allowed to stay, and not even certain what I was getting myself into.

I had so many preconceived notions of what making a movie would be like. I thought every moment would be exciting and assumed that all the scenes would be shot in sequence, starting at the beginning and finishing at the end. I had a great deal to learn, and *The Sound of Music* would be an education for me in more ways than I ever dreamed.

My indoctrination began the first moment I walked onto the sound-stage. I expected that we'd be filming in real houses, 'real' sets. But Soundstage 15 was an enormous, drab, dark, empty shell of a building. 'This is it?' I thought.

It wasn't until weeks later that I discovered that when a stage was 'hot,' and the cameras were rolling, everything came to life. The carbons of the arc lamp were struck against each other, making a light so bright that my eyes would water, and then the bell would ring, the assistant director yelled, 'Quiet on the set!,' and everything became perfectly still until Bob Wise called, 'Action!' A red light would flash off camera and the magic would begin.

It was all illusion, but for a moment it was real – the relationships, the story, the emotions – and when that moment was captured on film, it would become real for millions of people, too. Making the movie was an extraordinary experience. Dozens of people had to be in total concentration. It was never just the actor who brought enchantment to the screen – it was just the actor who got all the credit. But nothing happened without the cameramen and grips and gaffers and costume designers and makeup artists and sound technicians and production assistants. Together they made those electric moments happen. And those brief moments were what all of us working on *The Sound of Music* lived and breathed for.

But in the first days, before the cameras rolled and the soundstage came to life, there was a lot of work to do. From the moment I stepped onto Soundstage 15 in February of 1964, I was busy. We would begin principal photography in one month. During that short time we would have to not only learn our parts, including our lines and dances, but also prerecord the singing sound track.

On that first day, I received a copy of the whole script, and it was only then that I realized the extent of my role. I had no idea Liesl was a principal character, with her own story and romance. As I thumbed through the pages, all I could think was, 'This is going to be a lot of work.'

And it was. Every day we spent hours working on the songs and the dances and the dialogue. The professionals who helped us pull it all together were the tops in their fields: choreographers Dee Dee Wood and Marc Breaux (who had just finished *Mary Poppins*), vocal coach Bobby Tucker, music director Irwin Kostal, dialogue coach Pamela Danova, and of course our Oscar-winning associate producer, Saul Chaplin, and director, Bob Wise. There I was in my very first acting job, learning from the very best in the world. They made us all look good.

Julie and Chris and I were even given guitar lessons. None of us knew how to play, and we needed to look believable on camera. So Julie learned for 'Do-Re-Mi,' and Chris learned for 'Edelweiss,' and I learned for 'The Sound of Music,' which the children sing twice: first for the Baroness (with the Captain joining in part way through) and later for the Baroness and Uncle Max on the terrace. Though I enjoyed learning how to play – and a newspaper clipping from 1965 has me advising teens to 'pep up' their popularity by playing the guitar – I actually didn't continue after the filming ended. God forbid somebody should ask me to play the guitar at a party! Chris Plummer also retired as soon as the movie was complete. 'It was great fun to learn how to play,' he remembers, 'but it hurt my fingers too much.'

Pamela Danova was responsible for teaching us what she called a mid-Atlantic accent. Though we were playing Austrians, we were to speak in a cross between a British accent and an American one. We had to sound educated and aristocratic. I made careful notes on my copy of the script, notes that are still there in the margins and among the lines of dialogue. 'Father' was to be pronounced 'Fatha.' The long 'a' was eliminated from our vocabulary. 'France' became 'Frahnce.' The dialogue coach would have me repeat the same lines over and over until I got the sounds right. 'Where do you think we were, Father?'

'No,' Pamela would correct me. 'Eliminate the "r"s.'

I dutifully crossed out each and every 'r' in my script.

'Waya do you think we wu-a, Fatha?'

Before we ever went on location in Salzburg, we learned not only the dances, but the bike riding and the running that were to be part of the eleven-minute number 'Do-Re-Mi.' We practiced on bicycles on the back lot at Fox. I was grouped with Julie and Heather, and we had to time our riding and braking exactly together.

It was just one tiny segment of 'Do-Re-Mi,' but we spent a great deal of time practicing it. Every single frame of those eleven minutes was choreographed and rehearsed in Los Angeles. Saul Chaplin and Marc Breaux, armed with the recorded track of 'Do-Re-Mi,' had traveled to Salzburg and mapped out every move that would be done. Theirs was a perilous venture. With the sound track blaring, Saul and Marc had danced in Salzburg's busy streets, counting out the steps to each segment, as the traffic whizzed by them in both directions. Then they returned to Los Angeles to teach us the choreography they had designed.

Steps were built in Los Angeles, exact replicas of the ones in Salzburg, on which we practiced the grand finale of the song. Each step was numbered, and each child had a mark for each count, and his or her own note. Notes were assigned by birth order, descending from the high octave; so I was 'Ti,' Nicholas was 'La,' Heather was 'So,' Duane was 'Fa,' Angela was 'Mi,' Debbie was 'Re,' and Kymmie was 'Do.'

It took us days to master those moves on the steps. It's still one of the hardest dances I've ever done. Jumping backward was scary and took total concentration. And, of course, while we were jumping, we were also supposed to be singing in exact synchronization with the sound track. Getting that scene perfect required days of rehearsal and numerous takes.

'To this day,' Angela says, 'whenever I walk up to a set of wide steps like those in Salzburg, that music pops into my head. La-So, So-Fa, Mi-Re, Ti-Do! . . . It's ingrained!'

It was very strange practicing those pieces for 'Do-Re-Mi' in Los Angeles, because out of context they didn't make any sense. When we got to Salzburg and could see the actual locations, we began to understand a little. But we filmed the number bit by bit and still couldn't visualize how all those little pieces were going to fit together. We'd shoot five seconds of us patting a statue on the head. Then nine seconds of us running over a bridge. Four seconds marching around the rim of a fountain. Not until months later, when we saw the finished piece, did the flow of that sequence become clear.

Ernest Lehman, the film's screenwriter, should get a lot of the credit for opening up that musical number – in fact, for opening up the entire stage play. He himself says he feels that the 'Do-Re-Mi' montage is one of the happiest contributions he made to the film. In the original stage play, the entire song is sung in the von Trapp living room, which Ernie felt was too static a setting. Before sitting down to write the script, Ernie visited Salzburg, where he took note of the fabulous locations. He began to envision a sweeping scene that would highlight the Austrian landscape, use changes of costume and setting to indicate the passage of time, and show the evolution of Maria's relationship with the children. Ernie's vision coupled with Rodgers and Hammerstein's glorious music was spectacular on film.

The sound track was recorded before we ever shot a scene. With music director Irwin Kostal's guidance, we rehearsed each song for days before we recorded it with the orchestra. None of us playing the children had ever sung professionally before, and it took some getting used to. The songs were recorded in pieces. It was almost impossible to get all the singers and the orchestra perfect for a song of several minutes. We might record twenty bars, and then stop, and then pick it back up on bar fifteen. This didn't feel natural. To top it all off, we were wearing headphones inside a glass booth with the orchestra outside, and all the noise around us disappeared. Our job was to sing to what we heard, not to what we could see. And that's not as easy as it sounds.

A rumor started years ago that our voices were dubbed for the sound track. This is false. All the children who are in the film sing on the track. Four other children were added to most of the songs, to give us a fuller sound, but they were there to enhance the cast children's voices, not replace them.

Irwin Kostal taught me to act with my singing voice, even though I didn't quite know what the scenes would look like – we hadn't filmed them yet. When Christopher Plummer and I recorded 'Edelweiss,' I leaned forward in my chair in the glass recording booth, watching Chris, just as I would later do in the movie, a daughter at her father's knee, accompanying him in song. We acted out that entire scene in the recording booth, long before we ever did it in front of the cameras.

When the cameras finally did roll, we sang aloud to the sound track, trying to sync ourselves exactly to the track. Hundredths of a second were important, so the scenes that involved singing usually required many takes.

'Kymmie,' Bob would say to 'Gretl.' 'You're not singing.'

'Oh, I forgot.'

'Debbie,' he would say to 'Marta.' 'You're not supposed to be singing.' Debbie, a veteran of dozens of television commercials, knew everyone else's dialogue and lyrics, and would sometimes subconsciously help us along with our lines.

'Duane was making faces again,' Betty Levin, the script supervisor, would point out to Bob. Duane (Kurt) was always making faces or closing his eyes. He really *was* incorrigible at times.

Tomfoolery on the set, however, was rare. The children were extremely well behaved while working, and for the most part, things ran very smoothly. It was a charmed film from the beginning. As Saul would later say, 'It was the luckiest film I ever made.' All sorts of things could have gone wrong, but nothing insurmountable ever did. Over all the months of filming, not one child got sick. There was not a single attack of measles or mumps or chicken pox. No one even caught a cold. Which is not to say that there weren't certain challenges the children brought to the production that necessitated some creative solutions.

Debbie began to lose her baby teeth. A dentist was on call for such emergencies, and new temporary teeth would appear overnight. But Debbie hated those false teeth. 'They made me sound like I was lisping,' she remembers. 'That scene where I tell Maria my birthday's coming and I want a pink

44

parasol – those teeth made it hard for me to say the letter "s." And I wasn't supposed to say the "r" sound. I really had to concentrate to get the words out correctly.'

Because the film was a period piece, all of our costumes were custom-designed and hand-sewn. Costume designer Dorothy Jeakins said *The Sound of Music* was her all-time favorite project. 'I loved working on it. Bob Wise told me he didn't want saccharine costumes. He gave me a sense of the story's essence, and then he let me do my job. He was a wonderful director to work for.'

Over the course of seven months, children can grow. 'The children literally grew before my eyes,' remembered Dorothy. 'Especially Nicholas.' Nicholas Hammond grew six inches during the filming, from five foot three to five foot nine. His costumes were constantly being altered.

There was a last-minute decision to dye Nicky's hair. He was a brunet, and Bob decided at five-thirty the day before Nicky would go before cameras for the first time (to shoot 'My Favorite Things') that Friedrich should be blond. Back then the dyes they used to bleach hair were painful. As Nicky recalls, 'It was like having someone put a hot iron on my scalp. I sat there in the chair and just cried. By the next morning, when they began filming, the entire top of my head was covered with blisters. And if you look at that thunderstorm scene, my hair isn't totally blond yet. They had to keep lightening my hair the entire time we filmed, and I just hated it, because it hurt so bad.'

But he never complained, afraid they might hire someone else in his place. I think we all thought (especially in the early days of filming) that if we didn't do everything exactly the way they wanted, the studio would just hire other actors. I felt I could be gone in an instant, particularly before my screen test. And after two weeks of rehearsal, after falling in love with the script and the character and everyone who was working on the film, I knew if I wasn't permanently cast I was going to be devastated.

Finally, the day of my screen test arrived. At the time I was dating a young man named Mickey Levey. Mickey's dad, Harry, was one of my favorite people in the whole world. Perhaps because I hadn't seen my father since I was thirteen, my relationship with Harry was extremely important to me. He was always so supportive and humorous, and I adored him. He'd been encouraging me all week about my upcoming test: 'You're going to do fine, Charmy!'

But on the morning I was to face the camera, Thursday, February 27, Mickey called me. His father had had a massive heart attack. I got off the phone numb, and drove to the studio in a daze. I suppose it helped my screen test. I performed the dialogue from the gazebo scene, and I wasn't nervous at all. I could think about nothing but Harry.

I called Mickey as soon as I was done, and he told me his father had died. I couldn't believe it. I felt as if I had lost my own father.

When Saul Chaplin called me to tell me that my screen test was fine – I had passed and they would put me under contract, I was going to be Liesl – I didn't feel excitement or anything. On what should have been one of the most thrilling days of my life, all I could do was cry.

A woman raised in Grenada, now a research scientist in the United States, vividly remembers going to see The Sound of Music *in 1966.*

'Our entire school went,' she says. 'I was eight, and at an all-girls Catholic school run by nuns. My class had never gone on an excursion like that before, away from the campus, so it was very exciting. The nuns marched us in our white crisply starched blouses and blue skirts with tight pleats into the theater, and we took our seats.

'The lights dimmed, and suddenly the theater was pitch-black and the music began and the snow-covered Alps filled the screen. We were spellbound. We sat with our hearts racing, watching the scene with Liesl and Rolf, their teenage romance playing out our own future fantasies. It was beautiful – their dancing, the music. There we were on our island, from a different culture, even a different race, yet identifying with those children on the screen, because their story reflected our culture. Family is the backbone of life in the Caribbean. The story spoke our language.

'When the family climbs over the mountain in the final scene, there were so many emotions in the audience. Some girls were crying, even sobbing (we can cry really well in the Caribbean). Others were smiling, full of joy. All these emotions at the same time. The film said something different to each of us.

48

'I didn't understand the impact of the film then. But, looking back, it was a powerful event for me.

'It was the sixties, a time of change, a time of revolution, yet here was this hopeful story. The Sound of Music *told me that anything that seemed impossible was possible – if I had a family. I could triumph over any evil – even prejudice – as long as my family stood together.*

'It didn't tell me I needed technology to get ahead. It didn't tell me I needed something I didn't have. It told me the very tools I needed to succeed were within my grasp. They were right there when I opened the door to my home and raced into my mother's arms.'

DARK CHOCOLATE

We filmed the end of the movie near the beginning. After 'My Favorite Things,' we filmed the scene in the cemetery, where the family hides from the Nazis. The set really did feel like a cemetery, even though it was all fake, manufactured on a soundstage in southern California. It was dark and creepy and full of real-looking graves.

We were supposed to be anxious and terrified as we hurried behind the crypts to hide. But I found it difficult to feel as if we were being chased by Nazis. Here it was, the emotional climax of the film, and we hadn't done anything yet. I concentrated as hard as I could, but still wasn't sure I was bringing the emotions I should to the scene.

Nicky felt it was one of the few scenes in the film that required him to act. He had already worked on Broadway and in the film *Lord of the Flies*, and he wanted to be challenged as an actor. So he loved the cemetery scene. 'The thing I remember,' he recalls, 'is that I wanted to be able to stay on the set and hang out with all the adult actors. But our teacher, Frances Klampt, never let us stay on the set. During that scene in the graveyard, there were all these extras on hand, and I remember I was sitting in a chair just reading a book and being very bothered when Frances made me leave.

'There's stories and gossip – and language – that these people use that you shouldn't hear,' she said. She felt it was her job to protect us.'

Union regulations provided protection for the children in other ways as well. They had to be in school at least three hours daily, and were not allowed to work more than four hours during any given twenty-four-hour period. So our shooting schedule was built around the availability of the children, and often we had to stop in the middle of a scene and wait until the next day to finish because the four-hour limit had been reached.

The very first time the children were on camera was when we shot 'My Favorite Things' in Maria's bedroom, and it was one of my favorite scenes to film. Once I got past being drenched, and was dressed in one of Maria's dry nightgowns, that scene was fun. I felt very relaxed, partly because of the music, partly because of the choreography. In fact, the scenes in which we are singing and dancing were my favorite ones to work on. I never got tired of the sound track, of listening to it or of singing along to it.

Again, Ernie Lehman made a large contribution to improving the flow of the story. In the original play, 'My Favorite Things' is sung by the Reverend Mother to Maria before she leaves the abbey, and 'The Lonely Goatherd' is the song Maria sings to the children during the thunderstorm. I can't imagine how differently those two songs would have played in the film if Ernie had left them in that sequence.

It was Julie who put all the kids at ease during 'My Favorite Things.' It was their first scene, and they were as nervous as I had been coming through the window the day before. So, off camera, Julie made faces and funny noises, anything she could think of to break the tension. Her special efforts worked and encouraged us all to be playful and silly, just as the script calls for. We really *were* having fun.

During rehearsal, Dee Dee and Marc rechoreographed the pillow fight, transforming it from the dance they'd initially conceived into a frolic. *The Sound of Music* was only their second film (their first had been *Mary Poppins*), and Dee Dee said she learned a great deal from the scene in Maria's bedroom. 'We overstaged it. We choreographed each move, and it looked unnatural. That scene taught us simple is sometimes better. We gave the children only a few marks to hit, so that they'd really be playing with Julie. It looked much more natural on the screen than the original dance we had planned.'

Dee Dee has a wonderful memory of the first time Chris Plummer arrived to rehearse the Laendler, the folk dance that Captain von Trapp dances with Maria at the party he gives for the Baroness. Chris was supposed to meet with Dee Dee and Marc and Julie one morning at the rehearsal stage to begin learning the dance. He was a few minutes late, and when he arrived, they were all waiting for him. Dee Dee remembers turning, and then her jaw dropping wide open as Chris walked in the door – wearing tights and ballet shoes.

'I howled,' she remembers. 'Since he would be doing the dance in a captain's dress uniform, he didn't need to wear any unusual apparel to practice. But he did cut a fine figure in those tights.'

Chris went out of his way to bring humor to the set. 'Of course I got into tights and ballet shoes. It got a laugh. That was the whole point.'

Early in the filming in Los Angeles, Bob took me aside and told me something that young women in America rarely hear: 'Charmy, I want you to put on some weight.'

'What?'

'Liesl needs a little baby fat. It'll make you look younger.'

So, for the first time ever, I consciously tried to put on pounds. As Liesl, I weighed more than I ever have in my entire life, outside of my two pregnancies, and it was hard work to gain. But one scene actually helped.

After the cemetery set, we moved on to the dining room to film the scene in which Maria joins the family at dinner for the first time. Nicky remembers, 'They had us eating this appetizer when Maria arrived in the dining room. I had never had anything like it before. It was a roll of smoked salmon with cucumber in it. I thought it was terribly exotic. And we shot the scene over and over, so I got to eat a great deal of it.'

During the second part of the scene, we are eating dessert, a chocolate cake topped with whipped cream. That cake was so good. To this day, I can remember how it tasted. Again, we had to shoot the scene over and over, and I loved it. With each new take, a fresh piece of chocolate cake with heavenly whipped cream was placed before me on the table. I was gaining weight and working at the same time.

Our days in Los Angeles were so busy, they flew by. Before I knew it, the middle of April arrived and we were boarding a plane to fly to Salzburg, Austria. Ironically, my dream of traveling to Europe was coming true, and I can think of few times in my life when I've been as excited as when I boarded Pan Am flight 120 at twelve noon on Saturday, April 18, 1964. I'd been on a plane only once before in my whole life, a short flight from Los Angeles to San Francisco. Here I was, flying first class to London, Munich, and Salzburg.

I was like Maria leaving the abbey when I boarded that plane. I truly did wonder: What would this day be like? What would my future be? Where would this journey take me?

Before we even reached England, I knew that traveling would be something I would always enjoy. And when I first looked down on Salzburg from Winkler's Terrace, a stone walkway high above the city, I saw that it was just as I'd imagined a

European city to be, all cobblestone streets and slanted roofs.

I continued diligently on my mission to gain weight, and Salzburg was definitely the place to ensure my success. Between breakfast and lunch, the caterers would bring us sausages. Between lunch and dinner, they'd arrive with pastries. The cuisine was rich and addictive and, to make sure Liesl looked sixteen, I obediently ate everything. I willingly sacrificed my figure and set about consuming the food of Salzburg with a passion. I fell in love with Ice Café Mitschlags (vanilla ice cream mixed with espresso and whipped cream) and Salzburger Nockerls (enormous light soufflés filled with fruit) and cream soups and homemade breads with loads of sweet butter. I haven't bought a stick of salted butter since.

Then I found the one thing that would guarantee my success: dark chocolate. Ever since I was tiny, I had loved chocolate, milk chocolate. My favorite things were chocolate sodas and Hershey bars – these were the ways to my heart. But in Salzburg, I discovered a different kind of chocolate: European chocolate, dark and rich. I thought I'd died and gone to heaven. While the other actors sat around between scenes in Salzburg, fretting that they might be putting on too many extra ounces from all the rich food and frantically counting calories, I ignored their jealous glares and devoured Austrian and Swiss chocolate with reckless abandon.

To this day, I am addicted to dark chocolate. American milk chocolate hasn't done it for me since. Dark chocolate owns my heart. Perhaps it's because for me the taste is linked to such marvelous images. It conjures up Alps and lush meadows, cobblestone streets and slanted roofs, and something else: Being twenty-one and on my own in a European capital. The freedom I felt in Salzburg was intoxicating. Like my memories of making *The Sound of Music*, dark chocolate is one of the things I enjoy most in life.

*K*risten *is five.* The Sound of Music *is her favorite movie. Her parents can't say how many times she's seen the video. Still, they were surprised when Kristen announced that she wanted to be Liesl for Halloween.*

Both of her parents tried to discourage her. 'Honey, nobody's going to know who you are.'

'I don't care,' Kristen replied.

They took her to the Disney Store, hoping to entice her to choose something else. But Kristen wouldn't be deterred. 'I want to be Liesl.'

Her grandmother offered to make a dress exactly like the one Liesl wears when she dances in the gazebo. It turned out to be a much bigger project than she'd anticipated. Kristen went with her to pick out the fabric, and she was very particular. The dress had to twirl just like Liesl's, so the fabric had to be multilayered and fluffy.

'My mother-in-law made the dress without a pattern, simply by watching the film,' said Kristen's mother. 'She's very talented, but I don't think she planned on putting in sixty hours on a Halloween costume.'

The finished product was beautiful. Kristen put it on and mimicked the whole dance, all the while singing. She wore it in her very first Halloween parade.

'Who are you supposed to be?' other children asked.

'I'm Liesl,' Kristen answered, spinning around so that her dress would flare out. It didn't matter to her that a lot of her friends weren't sure who Liesl was.

It didn't end with Halloween, either. Kristen continued to wear the dress all the time. 'I've never seen anything like it,' says her mom. 'I mean, the movie is decades old, but Kristen relates to it strongly. It's the fantasy world she wants to live in. And she's worn that dress out. Her grandmother is currently repairing it so Kristen can wear it in a school play. That dress is timeless – just like the movie!' She laughs. 'It wouldn't surprise me at all if you asked her what she wanted to be when she grows up and she told you: Liesl.'

SHARON

As Liesl, I was the oldest. But in real life, that role was my sister Sharon's.

When I was small, and we were living in a butter-yellow brick house in Chicago, I would stand on tiptoe, a lipstick in my hand, trying to see my face in the mirror, and paint a line of red on my lips. 'Let me help you,' Sharon would say, lifting me up. Using a powder puff, she gently placed circles of pink blush on my cheeks, then did the same to herself, tottering in Mom's high heels.

'Here,' she'd say, 'wear this boa.' The feathers would encircle my neck and float down to the floor, and Sharon would step back and examine me. 'You're perfect.'

She'd step out from behind the makeshift theater curtain we'd hung in our living room to where our parents sat with a handful of their friends. 'Welcome,' Sharon began with a grand flourish, 'to our theater,' and her arm would sweep in my direction.

I would giggle and enter stage left, doing a ballet spin. I tried to balance on my toes as Sharon nodded at me, and the show would begin. We put on shows throughout our childhood. We did everything, making the stage, writing the script, creating our costumes, and performing for our parents and their friends. Darleen was born eight years after me; she could sing before she could even walk, and we immediately made her a part of the act. Our mother always sat in the front row, clasping her hands together and beaming at us. We were on stage, and she was right up there with us, willing us on.

My memories of childhood are happy. I was a very happy kid, a clown, always trying to be funny and whimsical. Sharon was the one who had to grow up too fast.

There were fun times with our parents. They would drive us out to the sand dunes on Lake Michigan, where we'd swim and have a picnic, or take us to the ice-cream stand that sold rainbow-sherbet cones.

But my most vivid childhood memories are of Sharon taking care of me. She insists that our mother was always there, too, and that we also had a woman named Johnny who baby-sat us, as well as our grandmother. But it is Sharon I remember who got me up every morning and made me breakfast and walked me to school, who led me down the sidewalk to the dentist's office when I was seven, who listened as the dentist explained that my back molars were decaying.

'They're just baby teeth,' the dentist, a friend of my mother's, told Sharon. 'She won't need them.' (Years later, a different dentist would confirm that those teeth were permanent molars and should have been filled, not extracted.) The dentist gave me laughing gas and pulled the teeth out;

afterward, Sharon took me home and nursed me through the rest of the day and night.

It was Sharon who helped me with math when I received a low mark in the fourth grade, who took me for sodas and chocolate turtles at the drugstore on the way home from school. She did everything to include me, playing with me, helping me cut out paper dolls and dress them in cut-out clothes, showing me how to fold down the paper tabs. We went to the movies together every Saturday. Doris Day movies were my favorite. Doris always seemed to be gazing out a window and singing a song.

'That's what I'm going to do,' Sharon would say. 'I'm going to be an actress like Doris Day.'

Such declarations always made Mom happy. She wanted us to reach for the stars, to follow in her footsteps and make a life for ourselves as performers. Mom had been on stage from the age of five, and she was a good teacher, coaching us in our homemade productions and helping us improve our skills. But we ultimately realized that it was not our success that our mother desired; it was applause for herself.

We moved from Chicago to the San Fernando Valley the summer I was thirteen. I hated leaving Chicago, leaving my best friends, leaving the yellow house where we'd had such good times. Sharon held my hand as we drove west – my friend as well as my sister. She would fill up the lonely spaces we encountered in our new home in California.

But before long, Sharon was made privy to the

fact that not all was happy in our household. 'Your father is a womanizer,' Mom told her one day. 'He's having an affair.' Polygamy would have suited my father. He didn't want to leave my mother – he just wanted to move his mistress in with all of us. When my mother, shock of shocks, declined this arrangement, he moved out.

Sharon's shoulder was the one our mother cried on. And so, after our father left, my sister not only took care of me, and later Darleen, she also took care of our mother. As a teenager, Sharon became the emotional foundation of our family.

I've often wondered who my mother might have been had my father stayed. All I know is bitterness consumed her in the years that followed. She began to do strange things, selfish things. With the three of us in the car, she'd drive over to the house our father had rented in Studio City to spy on him. We would sit in the car waiting for him to come outside. Sometimes she'd even make us sneak through the bushes to peer in his windows.

'Never, ever, under any circumstances, trust a man,' she would lecture us. She would drum this into our daily conversation until it became as natural as telling us to get ready for bed.

The way Sharon coped with all that was unraveling in our lives was to take total control of everything. She rebelled when she needed to, but she was very disciplined. She knew what she wanted to be: a successful actress. She had the talent and the drive to succeed, and she began to excel. In 1959, she was crowned 'Miss San Fernando.' Singing and dancing, she captivated everyone in the audience. The following year, she urged me to enter the contest. My own sister crowned me 'Miss San Fernando' for 1960. She was always looking out for me, always including me in her own activities and successes.

In retrospect, I am amazed by my sister. Every time Sharon accomplished something, it seemed I would follow. For some sisters, this shadowing might have destroyed their relationship. But not Sharon. She never stopped encouraging me.

When I was cast in *The Sound of Music*, my mother told me Sharon was devastated. I felt terrible, but I didn't talk to Sharon about it for years. My mother's comment ate at me. Sharon had worked so hard. She deserved to play Liesl, not me.

I would have saved myself years of guilt if I had discussed it with my sister back then. I should have known that Mom fabricated that story. Our mother's increasing bitterness – and her drinking – had given birth to many new traits, one of which was to divide and conquer her daughters. The older we became, the more we grew outside her sphere, the more she tried to push wedges between us. It was, I suppose, her way of having some control over us.

The truth was, Sharon might have been cast as Liesl if she had looked sixteen. She knew how to be an oldest sister! But she looked older and wiser than her years. She'd had too much responsibility too early to be able to pass for a naïve, wide-eyed girl. I stood behind my sister, protected in her wake from the abandonment and bitterness that swirled around us. In many ways, it was because of Sharon that I was ready for the opportunity to play Liesl.

Years later, I finally had the courage to ask Sharon if she had been hurt by my good fortune. 'No,' she said most emphatically, reaching for my hand. 'I admit I was stunned when you got picked, because there had been no visible desire on your part for such a lofty goal. But if it couldn't be me up there, I wanted it to be you.' And she squeezed my hand in her encouraging way. To encourage someone means giving the person hope and confidence. Sharon has always done this for me.

My older sister did fulfill her dream of becoming an actress. Her career spans almost four decades of theater and television and commercials. She never got the big break that I did in *The Sound of Music*; the film industry is fickle, and such opportunities are rare. But Sharon is a star. She is a star to me.

*S*ome people's stories can bring me to tears, like this one about a six-year-old named Abby.

'The Sound of Music *is her favorite movie,*' *her mother says. 'This year, Abby broke her collarbone, and when she came home from the emergency room, I rented her the video of* The Sound of Music. *She watched it three times in a row that day. As soon as it was over, she hit the rewind button and watched it again. It got her through that rough first day.*

'Ten days before Christmas, her brother had to have surgery, and we were at the hospital nonstop and didn't have time to prepare for the holidays. So one night I walked to a secondhand bookstore near the hospital to try to find a few presents for the kids. And there on a shelf was a very used copy of the Sound of Music *video for six dollars.*

'Our son was able to come home from the hospital on December 24, and so the whole family was together the next morning when Abby reached into her Christmas stocking. Inside was a single rectangular package. As she tore off the wrapping paper and saw what was in the box, Abby caught her breath. "Oh, wow, Mom! Look at this!" She held out the video, incredulous. "It's The Sound of Music! *It's just what I wanted! How did Santa know?!'*

'That day The Sound of Music *played over and over in our house. Abby watches it now at least once*

a week. It's hysterical to watch her watching the film. She begins on the couch. Then she inches forward. Every time there is a song, she jumps up and sings and dances. "Sixteen Going on Seventeen" is her favorite. By the time the movie is over she looks like she's going to crawl inside the television and join the von Trapps.

'She said that The Sound of Music was her favorite present, ever. It's just an old video of a movie that's five times older than she is. But to Abby, it's priceless.'

THE BRISTOL HOTEL AND
OTHER ADVENTURES

T he cast and crew of *The Sound of Music* took over four hotels in Salzburg. Julie stayed with her eighteen-month-old daughter, Emma Kate, at the Österreichischer-Hof with Saul and Bob, and I was put up at the Hotel Mirabell with all the other children and their mothers. But within days, Mike Kaplan, the film's publicist, moved me to the Bristol, where other members of the cast and crew were staying. I was thrilled. As much as I adored the children, at twenty-one I was an adult and wanted to be seen as one. It was during the evenings in the Bristol Hotel that I truly felt like a colleague of the older members of the cast.

Richard Haydn (Uncle Max) was so much fun. In casting the role of Max Detweiler, Bob and Saul had looked for a 'pixyish hand-kissing impresario who would sell his grandmother down the river only if he couldn't get more money *up* the river.' They had considered many other actors, including Walter Matthau, Robert Morley, Burgess Meredith, Jack Cassidy, Noël Coward, and Fred Astaire. But Richard Haydn, with his unique comedic timing and stately manners, brought just the right characteristics to the role that Bob Wise was seeking.

Richard had lived a fascinating life. He told us that he had gotten into acting because of a hurricane. 'I was a prosperous banana planter in the Caribbean,' he would say, then clear his throat. 'Well, at any rate, a banana planter. Along came a hurricane. When it was over, there was no plantation. I was left without a banana. There happened to be a film company shooting on the island. And, having nothing better to do that week, I became an actor.'

He was always telling jokes, and was very funny, very witty, but very much the British gentleman. People on the set would ask him to do his famous line from Disney's *Alice in Wonderland*. Richard had performed the voice of the Caterpillar in the animated classic, and one of his lines became a favorite in the sixties. The Caterpillar looks at Alice and says in a long-drawn-out voice, *'Who are you?'* Richard must have been asked to do that one line a hundred times. He was also famous for the character Mr Edwin Carp (immortalized on 'The Dick Van Dyke Show'), who could imitate the love call of a red-bellied gudgeon fish.

One day he got Eleanor Parker (the Baroness) to do the fish imitation with him. The sight of the two of them pretending to be fish, with their lips puckered out and their eyes crossed, was hysterical. It was doubly funny because Eleanor Parker was such an elegant woman. Portraying a red-bellied gudgeon was not something she would normally do, even though she was a versatile actress. She was the bona-fide movie star in the cast, with a career going back to the forties. Very pretty and pencil-thin, with slender arms and legs and a gorgeous face, she was a strong presence on the set and a class act. I was a little intimidated by her; this wasn't helped by one of the scenes we were in together.

While we were filming the scene in which the children and I are playing a game with the Baroness, throwing a ball back and forth, Bob directed me to throw the ball hard at Eleanor. I threw it much harder than Bob had intended me to, surprising myself with the force I used. I'll never forget the look on Eleanor's face when she caught that ball. I think she would have sent me to boarding school right then and there if she could have.

Nicholas remembers well the scene on the terrace in which the children learn of their father's engagement and have to kiss the Baroness. 'I really got into my role that day. I didn't want her to marry 'our father.' I remember giving her nothing in that kiss, telling myself that I should make it look like I was kissing a department-store mannequin.' Nicky succeeded in playing the scene perfectly, and Eleanor was superb. As the Baroness, she was the 'bad guy,' yet she brought such depth and dimension to the role that audiences respond sympathetically to her character. I've heard many people say, 'The Baroness wasn't the right woman for the Captain, but I really felt for her.'

There seemed to be two groups of actors on the set, the 'Hollywood' actors and the 'British' actors, and they pretty much stuck with their own. Richard was a part of the British group, which also included Julie and Christopher and Gil Stuart, who played the von Trapps' butler, Franz. Gil was a marvelous character actor, very reserved. Eleanor was part of the Hollywood group, which included actors like Ben Wright, who played Herr Zeller, and who would later lend his voice to the character of Grimsby in Disney's *The Little Mermaid*.

I adored the actresses who played the nuns, although I didn't get to know any of them very well because we weren't in many scenes together. Marni Nixon, who played Sister Sophia, was known for her work as a vocalist; she had dubbed some of the most prominent singing roles in movie history. Perhaps she is best known for *My Fair Lady*, in which she sang for Audrey Hepburn's Eliza. Many people felt that Julie Andrews, who had done the play on the Broadway and London stage, should have been cast in the film.

When Marni and Julie met for the first time on the *Sound of Music* set, everyone was concerned that Julie would be upset that Marni had a bit part in the film. But, surprising everyone, and setting a professional tone that would last for the entire picture, Julie just walked right over, put out her hand, and said, 'Marni, I'm such a fan of yours!'

Anna Lee, who played Sister Margaretta, had known Nicky's mom from their days in the British theater, and the two of them had fun reminiscing while we were in Salzburg. Portia Nelson – who, like me, was making her film debut in *The Sound of Music* – had a commanding presence as Sister Berthe. She was very tall and had a powerful voice so you always knew when she was on the set.

Peggy Wood, who played the Reverend Mother, was one of the loveliest women I have ever met. I felt more honored to be in a film with her than with any of the other actors. Julie and Chris were stage actors, and I had never been exposed to any of their work. But it was a thrill for me to walk onto the set with the star of the television show 'I Remember Mama,' which I had watched faithfully when I was younger. All the beautiful qualities of the Reverend Mother were there inside Peggy Wood; she was gracious and lovely and wise. I was in only a couple of scenes with her – early in the filming, when we were hiding in the graveyard, and later, when the von Trapp children come to the gate of Nonnberg Abbey looking for Maria – but whenever I got to be on the set with her, I basked in her warmth.

I remember being fascinated by how the makeup artists taped back the skin of Peggy's face before she put on her nun costume. It was like an instant face-lift. I always wondered if it hurt. But it gave her face a beautiful fan of smile wrinkles that seemed to be replicated by the folds of her wimple, particularly when she is softly lit for 'Climb Ev'ry Mountain.'

Of all the adult actors and actresses associated with the film, the one I most enjoyed getting to know was Christopher Plummer. My first impression of Chris had been: How veddy British. Like

Julie, he displayed an English reserve. Actually, he's Canadian, born and raised in the Laurentian Mountains, north of Montreal. Ironically, as a boy, he had visited the Trapp Family Lodge in Stowe, Vermont, while vacationing with his mother. 'I've skied all my life,' says Chris, 'and remember going to Stowe on holiday. I didn't meet Baroness von Trapp face to face back then, but I distinctly remember seeing her from a distance.'

They finally met on the set in Salzburg and would grow quite fond of each other. 'She was naughty and funny and just a delightful person,' Chris remembers. 'She was very sweet to me, always.' He smiles. 'She had this laugh like a German *Hausfrau*. 'Ho, ho, ho,' she'd say. "*Ach*, Christopher, you're so much more handsome than my real husband. Ho, ho, ho." God love her, she was fun.'

The friendship between Chris and the real Baroness von Trapp would continue long after the movie was made. 'We'd cross paths every so often. I met her once down in Nassau when I was on vacation with my cousin. She was quite famous as a long-distance swimmer, and it just so happened when I was in Nassau Maria was also there, swimming the Nassau Channel.' He laughs. 'It was marvelous. Here was this wonderful rotund woman with all these little boats following her, and people throwing her bananas to eat during her crossing. It was quite something. We arranged to meet later at the hotel. She had this wild humor and absolutely no pretensions of grandeur at all. She arrived with the governor general of Nassau, and everyone was being very stuffy and prim, and Maria saw me across the room and shireked, "My husband! My husband!" and came running over to me, giving me this huge bear hug embrace. I absolutely adored her.'

Christopher came to *The Sound of Music* from the theater. Robert Wise had seen him on stage in New York and felt Chris would bring a needed depth to the role of the Captain. But Chris hesitated. More suited to roles like Hamlet and Iago and Henry V, he wasn't at all interested in the part when Bob first called him. Bob flew all the way to London to try to persuade him, telling him how right he'd be for the role, how much he would add. His agent thought it was a good opportunity for him, and Chris did like the idea of a singing role. But still he was reluctant.

Of course, although Bob was absolutely certain he wanted to cast Chris, the higher-ups at Twentieth Century Fox thought he was too young for the part. The Captain was supposed to be a 'tall aristocratic man of 40–45.' Christopher was only thirty-four; it has always struck me as amusing that I was too old to be Liesl, and Chris too young to be the Captain.

The studio wanted to do a screen test of him to make sure that he could look the part of a retired submarine captain. Chris refused to test. He told Bob if they wanted him he was willing to sign on, but he wasn't about to audition for the film. All he would agree to was having some still photographs taken of him after he'd been 'aged' by a makeup artist. Apparently he proved he could look the part, because Bob Wise was at long last able to sign the actor he had wanted to play Captain von Trapp.

Whether he truly wanted to be in the film or not, Christopher did add a great deal to *The Sound of Music*. To understand his contribution fully, one must see the original stage version of the story. The weakest character in the whole play is the Captain, who comes off as passive and undefined. Chris says, 'I'd seen the play on Broadway and knew it wasn't a part I wanted to do. Theodore Bikel played the Captain on stage, and the way it was written, every time Theodore opened his mouth to say something, Mary Martin would sing fourteen verses of a song and drown him out. Here was this man, this great actor, and he had nothing to do.' Chris pauses. 'Also, I knew a little bit about the Baroness [von Trapp]. I hadn't met her yet, but I'd seen her and I knew she couldn't have married a dull man. She had too much humor and too much of a spark inside her. Her husband had been a man of strength. And in the stage play, he wasn't portrayed that way.'

Christopher Plummer would ultimately bring an edge to the role, a depth to the character – not to mention sex appeal – that helped make the film much more powerful. Nowhere are his contributions more evident than in a letter he wrote to Bob Wise in February of 1964, after he had signed on to do the picture. Bob had encouraged Chris to write down the changes he envisioned making in the character, and he got more than he bargained for when Chris sent him several pages of suggestions.

He [the Captain] is far more sophisticated and cultured a man than the script so far suggests. Underneath his hard unbending exterior lies a strong dis-satisfaction with both himself and his life – this he attempts to camouflage with a sharp mind and a sardonic wit . . . He must not appear – as in other productions – in any way a pushover. There must be a real fight between him and Maria . . .

Another great opportunity for some wit is in his attraction for Elsa: it would be delightful if their dialogue throughout could sparkle along with more edge and style than in the current script. This would heighten . . . the scene where he tells Elsa he can't marry her, being suddenly rendered speechless in contrast to their easy, flowing, glib relations of before.

Chris ended his letter with an interesting comment.

I'm afraid I don't like the song 'Edelweiss' period. I suppose it's unavoidable but, as it's my only solo, I hope something can be done about it since it's very boring, schmaltzy and trite . . .

Bob Wise immediately wrote him back and said, 'Sorry to hear your reaction to "Edelweiss" – but I'm afraid it's a must in the picture . . . I don't think there will be an opportunity for a new song as a solo for you. The script is already pushing the limits for length.' I find it ironic that though he hadn't liked 'Edelweiss,' Chris indicated strong enthusiasm for the song 'An Ordinary Couple' – which was ultimately cut from the picture.

Ernest Lehman was one of the most famous and successful film writers of the time, with tremendous credits to his name, such as *Sabrina*, *Executive Suit*, *Somebody Up There Likes Me*, *Sweet Smell of Success*, and *North by Northwest*, as well as the screenplays of *The King and I* and *West Side Story*. When Bob Wise called him about Chris Plummer's concerns, Ernie certainly didn't have to listen to Chris or incorporate any of his suggestions. But he did. He listened to them all.

Ernie had long had a reputation for being inflexible about his scripts. To him, they were *final*. Perhaps Ernie was willing to bend a little for Chris because he himself loved the project so much. In fact, *The Sound of Music* might never have been made, much less been as good as it was, if not for Ernie Lehman.

Ernie remembers, 'When I saw the play in New York during the second week of its run, to less-than-ecstatic reviews, I told my wife during the intermission, "I don't care what anyone says: someday this could make a very successful movie."'

He didn't tell just his wife. He also said the same thing to his friend David Brown, vice-president at Twentieth Century Fox, who made Ernie repeat the prediction to then studio head Buddy Adler. Fox had an option on the play, and soon thereafter exercised it.

Still, not many people shared Ernie's enthusiasm for the project. Burt Lancaster walked by Ernie's table in the Fox commissary one day and asked, 'What are you doing here, Ernie?'

'I'm writing the screenplay for *The Sound of Music*.'

'Jesus,' Burt said, rolling his eyes. 'You must really need the money!'

Billy Wilder, with whom Ernie had done *Sabrina*, said, 'I hear you're working on *The Sound of Music*.'

'That's right.'

'My dear boy,' Billy said, shaking his head sadly, 'no musical with a swastika in it can ever be successful.'

Even Ernie's agent at William Morris was opposed to his doing the project and tried to discourage him from taking it on. But Ernie loved the soul of the story and the music. Nothing was going to dissuade him. And so, with the Broadway cast album playing continually on the record player in his office, Ernie hunkered down and wrote a terrific script.

Saul Chaplin, who would eventually become such a creative force on the film, was totally uninterested in the project at first. He was asked to read Ernie's screenplay to see if it might be an appropriate project for Bob Wise. As Saul himself later recalled, 'If ever there was a chore I didn't want to fulfill, this was it. I had seen the play on the stage and hadn't liked it. So I was being asked to read the screenplay of a show I didn't like. Halfheartedly, I agreed to read it as a favor to Bob.'

Before he even sat down to read the script, Saul was thinking of things to say to Bob to convince him not to do the film: 'It's a helluva job Ernie did, but it's still too saccharine.' Or: 'It's an improvement over the play, but it's still not for you.'

But then he read Ernie's screenplay. 'I was never so happy reading a script in my life,' Saul would later write. 'It was wonderful.' He not only encouraged Bob to do the film, but later signed on himself.

When Bob Wise called Ernie to ask if he'd be willing to make some changes in the script for Chris, Ernie recalls, 'I was already working on *Who's Afraid of Virginia Woolf?* at Warner Bros., but I said, Sure, I'll talk to the guy.'

Ernie laughs. 'Chris didn't sit down for four days! He paced the floor of my office. I was like one of the von Trapp children. But I give him a lot of credit. He's an intelligent actor, and his suggestions were extremely helpful. He made me make it a better picture.'

Chris laughs, too, as he remembers the romantic visions he'd had of himself and Ernie, closeted away, revising the script. 'Ernie didn't smoke, and I was disappointed. I had envisioned the two of us in this smoky room, like two old screenwriters put together. Very Heming-wayesque. But even though it wasn't that type of atmosphere, I think between the two of us we made the Captain a much more believable and real character.'

It is no secret that Chris didn't interact much with the children. He was distant, if not outright aloof, in his off-screen dealings with most of them. Heather says that, during the entire seven months of filming, he never said a single word to her off camera. Not one.

Angela shrugs. 'He was always nice to me, but he could be distant. Who knows? Maybe it was a conscious decision by Chris to be that way. Maybe it was some kind of Stanislavsky thing and he was staying in character.'

Whatever his intention, Chris treated the child actors much the same way that Captain von Trapp treated his children in most of the script, keeping them at arm's length. If his behavior was intentional, it certainly worked in the film.

Some felt that Chris acted as if *The Sound of Music* was beneath him. He was never a strong promoter of the film, and even though he denies having ever called it 'The Sound of Mucus,' I think he did view the whole enterprise, at least back then, as lacking depth. His behavior on the set ruffled many people, especially Saul Chaplin, who, though he valued Chris's contribution to the movie, was more than irritated by him. Saul once wrote of Chris, 'He behaved as though he were a distinguished legendary actor who had agreed to grace this small amateur company with his presence.' Even if there was no love lost between them, Saul also complimented Chris as a fine actor, who was always professional on the set and contributed to the success of the film.

The tension between Saul and Chris was certainly exacerbated by Chris's anger when he was told his singing would be dubbed for the film. He was interested in doing a musical version of *Cyrano de Bergerac* on the stage and felt doing a musical film would be an excellent way to prepare. But before we even began shooting, he learned that Saul and Bob planned to use a voice double for him, and he threatened to walk off the picture.

Dorothy Jeakins was working on the master fittings for the costumes when Chris came over and whispered to her, 'Don't go too far with your work on my costume. This may all blow up.'

Years later, Dorothy would say, 'Can you imagine if he hadn't done the film what would have happened? We were starting principal photography the following Monday! All the time and effort and money that would have been lost if he had walked.'

Negotiations began between Chris and Bob and Saul and studio vice-president Dick Zanuck. Finally, it was agreed that Chris would prerecord the original sound track. It would be the playback he sang to in all the scenes during filming. Then, when postproduction began, Chris himself would decide if his voice held up.

'He had a good voice,' said Saul. 'But the script called for him to have a great voice. He was singing opposite Julie Andrews, for Chrissakes.'

Chris counters, 'Julie Andrews sang on stage opposite both Rex Harrison and Richard Burton, and neither of them could sing a note!' Still, after principal photography ended, Chris ultimately gave in and agreed that a dubbed voice would be better than his own, so a professional singer named Bill Lee was brought in to rerecord the Captain's numbers during postproduction. Since our voices were on separate tracks, Bill sang along to the prerecorded versions, and I think he did a wonderful job of matching Chris on the screen. But the whole process was laced with irony for Chris, since singing in the film was one of the reasons he'd agreed to do the picture in the first place.

In 1996, Twentieth Century Fox digitally remastered the sound track and invited me to the sound studio to listen. While I was there, they played the original recording of the duet Chris and I had done of 'Edelweiss.' I had always felt Chris had a fine voice, and had never really understood why Saul and Bob were so adamant about dubbing him – until that day. As I listened to Chris's track, and then Bill Lee's, I was at last convinced that the proper decision had been made.

By the time we arrived in Salzburg, Chris was

totally committed to the film. Any frustrations he still had, he saved for the piano in the Bristol's lobby. Every night, without fail, once the dinner dishes had been cleared away and a round of after-dinner drinks consumed, Chris would commandeer the upright piano in the lobby of the Bristol and begin to play. He played from memory, improvising a lot, and the more intoxicated he became, the better the piano sounded. I was delighted when he invited me to join in these late-night piano recitals. Wide-eyed and twenty-one, unlike Liesl in the film, I got to taste my proverbial (and literal) first champagne.

We would stay up late into the night, along with Eleanor Parker and Pamela Danova and Dee Dee Wood and other members of the cast and crew, and the many locals whom Chris had befriended. Dee Dee remembers, 'He taught us all how to drink during those days in Salzburg. He introduced me to this liqueur called "William's Pear." A pear is actually grown inside the bottle, and then the sugar in it is distilled. It's yummy – and strong. Chris taught us how to drink it from these little glasses. I still have the bottle of "William's Pear" I bought in Salzburg in 1964. I take it out every now and then and have a little sip, and it always makes me think of Chris Plummer and staying up late into the night at the Bristol Hotel.'

I don't think Bob Wise ever knew how late we were up. It was often past midnight, and we had a 5:00 A.M. wake-up call. But no one ever arrived hungover, and no one ever botched his or her lines.

To me, Chris Plummer was tremendous fun. He was outrageous and complicated and always made me laugh. We were only thirteen years apart in age, and he was terribly handsome and dashing, and as flirtatious with me as I was with him.

It's funny now to think of someone else playing the Captain. Initially, the studio had wanted Bing Crosby. Bob Wise said, 'No way.' All along he was thinking of Chris, whom he had seen on the New York stage. Still, others were considered before Chris was put under contract, including Rex Harrison, Richard Burton, Peter Finch, David Niven, Edward Mulhare (who would later play a different captain on the television show 'The Ghost and Mrs Muir'), Louis Jordan, Maximilian Schell, Brian Keith, Paul Scofield, Yul Brynner, and Sean Connery. (Now, I wouldn't have minded working with *him*.)

I loved working with Chris. He was acerbic and sarcastic, but always humorously so. Without him, the long days of filming would have been dreary. He added so much liveliness to the days on location. And he made a conscious effort to do so. 'God, it could have been so deadly dull,' says Chris now. 'Filming *The Sound of Music* was like acting out the Lord's Prayer every day. It was absolutely my intention to play at the absurd. To be irreverent. I felt if I didn't, if we took our roles too seriously, the whole thing was going to come off schmaltzy.'

So, every morning, as Julie and Chris and I had our makeup done in the same room in the Bristol, Chris would arrive grumbling and swearing: '*Ach!* We're not going to work today. It's raining. Why the hell do we have to go through the paces when we know we're not going to do anything? Bloody hell!' Every morning his tirade made me laugh.

He told publicist Mike Kaplan, 'It's ridiculous to have to sit around waiting when they know it's not going to stop raining. There's just nothing to do while we wait out the weather. We've tried reading, but we've run out of material. The other day I found our English camera assistant avidly reading the instructions on a box of German soap powder someone had on the set – and the guy can't speak a word of German. That's how bad it is.'

Sometimes, he would bring his crusty complaining to the set. While we were filming the very final scene, in which we walk up over the mountain and Captain von Trapp is carrying his youngest daughter piggyback, Chris wasn't shy about making his sentiments known when he was asked to carry her for more than one take.

Kymmie was an adorable and very self-assured little girl. I always used to tell people that, even though her birth certificate said she was five, she was really forty-two. She would climb up into my lap and squish my cheeks together as if she were my grandmother and say, 'Oh, I just love your dimples! You're so cute!'

Adorable as she was, Kymmie was not a light-weight back then, and the food in Salzburg made things worse. When we were in Los Angeles in the spring, rehearsing 'So Long, Farewell,' and I picked her up and carried her up the stairs at the end, I thought, 'Wow, she's heavier than she looks.' That scene wasn't filmed until months later, in late July, after we'd returned from our location shooting in Salzburg. Having consumed all those Salzburg desserts and her favorite, fried artichoke hearts, Kymmie seemed to have gained twenty pounds. I look at that scene and think, 'Hey! I can act!' There's not even a tiny grimace to show how hard it was for me to lift Kymmie and carry her up those stairs. Still, if you watch my steps once I reach the top landing, you can tell that I am struggling to hold her. By the end of that day on the set, I thought my arms were going to fall off. But I never dreamed of saying anything about it.

Chris Plummer, on the other hand, when he was called upon to carry Kym piggyback up that mountain ridge one more time, didn't mince words. 'Another take?! Not again! I can't carry that kid one more step up this mountain. She's built like a bloody tank!' (Today Kym is gorgeous and trim and looks like a model, and I'm sure Chris wouldn't mind carrying her anywhere for a few takes . . .) For the long-distance helicopter shots of that final scene, they ended up using a double who was lighter and easier for Chris to carry up the steep trail.

Twentieth Century Fox was on the verge of

bankruptcy while we were filming *The Sound of Music*. *Cleopatra*, which cost more than forty-two million dollars, had turned out to be one of the biggest bombs in film history, and in 1963 the studio was finally forced to sell off most of its backlot (today known as Century City). Fox was rolling the dice on *Music*. If it flopped, the studio would cease to exist. So, throughout the filming, Bob was constantly looking at his pocket watch, trying to be as efficient as possible and not waste a minute of time. Despite all his best efforts, circumstances outside his control would bog the production down. Our shoot in Salzburg was supposed to last only six weeks, but it stretched to ten.

Since the studio had to pay each actor a per diem for each day on location, Bob worked hard to finish all the scenes for specific actors and send them home. Julie would be in Salzburg for the entire time, as would the children and I. But Chris Plummer was not. He finished in mid-June, and one day he was simply gone. Salzburg wasn't the same after he left. Of course, we would see him again when filming resumed in Los Angeles. But spending time with Chris Plummer was, like dark chocolate, one of my favorite memories of those days in Salzburg.

I saw Chris recently doing *Barrymore* on stage in Los Angeles. He was phenomenal, his performance riveting. Afterward, I went backstage to say hello. He was still the same old Chris, crusty and irreverent and, in the theater, very much a man in his element.

'Why don't you come visit me at the Bev Hills, love,' he said, with that half-smile of his.

'I will,' I promised, 'as long as you'll be playing the piano.'

He beamed. 'Of course.'

I like to envision visiting Chris in his suite. He'll be playing some improvisational composition, with a group of friends gathered round, a glass of schnapps perched on top of the piano for inspiration. Making his own music.

*D*ear Mom and Darleen, *May 15, 1964*
Thank you for your letters. It rained today so we didn't shoot and since we didn't have a cover set we are behind another day . . .

May 21, 1964
Dan (Rolf) and I are in my trailer singing. It rained again today but we did some shots in the morning, but had to quit in the afternoon so I went shopping for bubble bath and toothpaste (they don't have any Crest!) . . .

May 25, 1964
We are in a new location today – the Trapp Villa – where Rolf and I do our scenes – and it is simply gorgeous. There is a beautiful lake right in the back of the gardens that Dan and I went rowing on today during lunch – it was smooth as glass.

I guess in a way my life is just beginning. Whenever I think about all that has happened in the past 4 months and all that will be happening in the future, I get butterflies in my stomach.

I wish you could be here with me. The river is so inspiring and the trees are tall and green – all pointing up to God. I wish I could stay here forever. It is almost like being in Heaven. Up in

*these mountains I wish I could take a deep breath
and soar up over the trees and mountains and glide
down into the valleys and take in all the beauty at
once . . .*

Love,
Charmy

THE HILLS ARE ALIVE

There's a reason the hills and meadows look so lush and green in the film: it rained almost every day. The information sheet we were given before the trip had suggested we bring raincoats and rain shoes: 'It is known to rain in Salzburg.' That was the biggest understatement of the year. The rain was unrelenting and added weeks to our shooting schedule. At times, it was like being prisoners of the weather. Every day we had to be prepared to shoot, even if it was pouring at our 5:00 A.M. wake-up call. We'd be in costume for hours, ready to go, waiting and waiting either for the clouds to clear or for Bob to cancel the shoot for the rest of the day.

Julie never seemed bothered by all the delays. Chris would swear. And Bob, who knew what was on the line as each minute ticked by, never lost his cool. Each successive day put his film further and further over budget. But, except for one single instance, he never let us see the strain he was under. Ever the perfectionist, he worked until he got each and every shot exactly the way he wanted it, and if that meant waiting patiently for clouds to clear and the wind to die down, so be it.

The one time I saw Bob lose his patience was on the very first day we filmed in Austria. We were far from Salzburg, in the village of Mondsee, a town as magical as something out of a fairy tale. There, in the cathedral where the real Maria and Georg von Trapp had been married, we filmed the wedding scene. To me, it's one of the most beautiful moments in the entire movie.

Betty Levin, the script supervisor, was seated on the camera dolly with Bob as the cameras began to roll. Julie followed me up the aisle toward Chris, who was waiting at the top of the steps. It was all picture-perfect – and then Bob looked through the lens and realized there was no priest standing at the altar. 'Cut!' he yelled.

Everyone was a little on edge, because it was the first day on location, the first scene. I guess Bob took out his anger on Betty because she was seated next to him; it was not solely her responsibility to make sure the priest was there. Julie later said she'd never heard anything as icy as Bob's voice when he took Betty to task that day.

Back then, Betty was called a 'script girl.' She'd worked on everything from 'The Mickey Mouse Club' to *The Americanization of Emily,* and more recently has supervised films like *Private Benjamin* and *Outrageous Fortune.* I was fascinated by her job. She had to watch every scene for continuity, monitoring every gesture, every expression, every piece of clothing, everything down to the way each actor's hair was combed. Her job was to make sure every single detail matched in each shot so the different takes would blend together when the film was edited. If the details in a scene didn't match, it was Betty who took the blame.

The Sound of Music must have been a nightmare, what with scenes featuring ten characters or more, many of them children. Betty's copious notes and comments on her working script reveal the details that she was responsible for observing during each take.

> *Kurt not singing.*
> *Children out of line.*
> *Louisa – hair funny.*
> *Marta – out of sync.*
> *Gretl – late.*

Invariably, her notes would read, 'Maria – very good!' The adults had to be perfect in every take, because, with so many children in a scene, the odds were that one of them might miss a mark. Out of several takes there might be only one in which all of the children were perfect, so the adults couldn't afford to make a mistake during any take.

Betty was a hard worker, and also a loner. She'd frequently be off at her portable desk, typing away, reviewing her notes. She liked a quiet set. Saul Chaplin drove her nuts. Always jolly, he loved playing with the kids. He'd get them all wound up, and they would be laughing and jumping up and down. Saul was also the associate producer, which was a very powerful position. Today it is a less impressive title, but back then the associate producer played a critical role that entailed a lot of creative input. Still, powerful or not, he annoyed Betty so much that one day she'd finally had enough. 'You're too noisy!' she snapped. Well, that got Saul's attention.

We all watched as it happened. Saul and Betty fell in love in Salzburg. Actually I think it started way back in Los Angeles, at the beginning of filming, when I was supposed to come in that window. During the rehearsal for that scene, the lightning and thunder were being cued on the set. And after each bolt of lightning flashed, Saul could hear counting: 'One thousand one, one thousand two, one thousand three.' It would stop as soon as the thunder began.

'What the heck is making that sound?' he asked.

It was Betty, counting between the lightning and thunder to see how far away the 'storm' was. I've always thought that endeared her to him.

In Salzburg, Saul invited Betty, along with a number of other people, to attend a series of chamber-music concerts. Soon it was just the two of them going. Saul would take four years to muster the courage to ask her to marry him, but their romance began during long walks along the banks of the Salzach River.

The rest of the shoot inside the church in Mondsee went smoothly, and we managed to complete all of those shots in just one day. I remember it so well, the beauty of the church inside and out. The village of Mondsee is in the middle of a lake at the base of sheer cliffs; it is one of the most enchanting spots on earth. The majesty of the moment when we filmed the wedding is a very clear memory for me – as is how cold we all were. It was freezing inside that church. We simply couldn't get warm. Chris was irreverently funny the entire day. 'It's bloody freezing in here,' he'd remark. 'It's colder than a witch's tit!'

But as I walked down the aisle ahead of Julie, I forgot all about being cold. The whole moment was so breathtaking, it took my mind off everything else. It was simply spectacular.

Julie's dress was elegant but quite heavy, with a fourteen-foot train. It took her half a day to learn how to navigate the aisle and the steps with it, not to mention kneel at the altar. She never complained. I remember hearing about the day they filmed the song 'I Have Confidence.' Marc Breaux, one of the choreographers, cavorted down the dirt lane toward the Trapp Villa, showing Julie the steps she was to do. She'd already practiced them in L.A., so she was ready to go after just a couple of rehearsals. A truck with the camera drove ahead of Julie. On the first take, the guy driving the truck went too fast, and Julie couldn't keep up. Something else ruined the second shot, and then the third one was spoiled at the very last moment when the cameraman's hat blew off and landed right in the middle of the road, where Julie stepped on it. She would have to do yet another take, but she just trotted right back to her starting mark and began again. She was never grumpy, always willing to go for as long as it took to get a scene right.

I have to believe those months in Salzburg were difficult for her. Her husband at the time, Tony Walton, was doing a show in New York and couldn't join her, and Julie had their very young daughter with her throughout. She had a lot to juggle, but her star was rising, though none of us knew that when we were in Salzburg. *Mary Poppins* hadn't even been released yet. None of us had seen her work on stage.

None of us, that is, except Nicky. 'Friedrich' was the only one who was starstruck by Julie's presence. His mother was English and had been an actress before marrying his father, and when Nicholas was nine years old, she took him to see Julie Andrews and Rex Harrison performing *My Fair Lady* on the London stage. It was his first exposure to the theater, and as he watched Julie Andrews walk out on stage in the first act, Nicholas Hammond decided then and there that he was going to be an actor.

So Nicky was absolutely in awe when he finally met her. He kept saying to the rest of us, 'Don't you realize who this is?' We would soon find out. Within less than twelve months, Julie would earn the Oscar for Best Actress for her performance in *Mary Poppins*.

But even if I didn't know who Julie Andrews 'was' during our days shooting the film, I was always impressed by her ability, as well as Chris's, to find the right emotions on camera. One morning on location at the private estate called Frohnburg (which served as the front and part of the back of the Trapp Villa), they filmed the scene in which a soaking-wet Maria shouts at the Captain ('I am not finished yet, Captain!' – to which he replies, '*Oh yes you are*, Captain!'). Later that very same day, Chris and Julie (and all of us) filmed the scene in front of the house in which Maria and the Captain return from their honeymoon, and he tears down and rips up the Nazi flag. Those two scenes represent entirely different moments in the film and require entirely different moods, yet Julie and Chris capture them perfectly.

Two different locations were used for filming the back of the Trapp Villa, which made for some tricky camera angles and acting. Frohnburg was used for the actual house – but not the terrace and the lake. Scenes with that backdrop were filmed at another location, a house known as Bertelsmann. For the scenes that show both the back of the house and the lake with its terrace, we had to act (and film) in both locations. For example, when Maria is shouting at the Captain on the terrace, Julie is standing on the steps at Frohnburg. But when the Captain responds to her, Chris is on the set at Bertelsmann. These scenes weren't the only ones that used two different sets. Portia Nelson always joked that when the Nazis rang the bell at Nonnberg Abbey, she walked all the way from Los Angeles to Salzburg to answer that bell, for it was filmed both on a soundstage at Fox and on location in Austria.

Some of the loveliest nighttime scenes in the film were actually shot during the daytime on the terrace at Bertlesmann. When Liesl runs across the terrace to meet Rolf after dinner, that was filmed in broad daylight using a 'day-for-night' filter on the camera lens. And the scene in which the Captain watches Maria on the terrace from his balcony was shot using the same technique (though the balcony was on a soundstage in Los Angeles).

In Salzburg, I would learn that filming on location could be much more difficult than filming on a soundstage. There were many distractions and problems that couldn't be controlled. If a plane went by overhead, you had to stop and wait. If a car backfired, you had to reshoot the scene. Anytime there was any ambient sound, we would do another take. Often, gawkers would cause problems. People would interrupt us to find out what we were doing. Onlookers were supposed to stay behind barriers, but I recall more than one instance when someone interfered with a scene and we had to do another take.

So it was a great relief when we got to go into the countryside one day to shoot the little 'Do-Re-Mi' segment in which we are on bicycles. We went to a beautiful spot on the edge of a lake, with no one around at all. It's only a tiny piece of film but a big memory for me, because it was so much fun to do, and so relaxing to be away from the crowds.

Two scenes that we shot in Salzburg ended up

not being used in the final cut of the film.

The first was a short segment with Liesl and Rolf (Daniel Truhitte) in downtown Salzburg, right in the middle of the 'Do-Re-Mi' sequence.

> LIESL

Hello, Rolf . . .

> ROLF
>
> (staring at her costume)

Hello . . .

> LIESL
>
> (eagerly)

Would you like to go on a picnic with us?

> ROLF
>
> (coolly)

Picnics are for children. And so is that . . .
> (gesturing at her costume)

Liesl then introduces Rolf to Fraulein Maria, who is standing nearby with the other children.

> MARIA

I'm Fraulein Maria . . .

> LIESL
>
> (hastily)

The governess of my brothers and sisters.

> MARIA
>
> (with a knowing glance at Liesl)

That's right. Liesl's *friend*.

(awkwardly)
Yes ... uh ... well ... I have to be
going ...

Bob and Saul ultimately decided that this exchange
broke up the flow of the musical piece, and they cut
it.

The other scene that didn't make it into the film
involved Maria and the Captain. After the Captain
sings 'Edelweiss' to his children, and the Baroness
senses that something is happening between the
Captain and Maria, she suggests that he host 'a
grand and glorious party for me.' In the film, after
the kids dash off to bed in excitement, there is an
immediate segue to the grand event. But the script
called for two short scenes before the party.

Alone now, [the Captain] starts slowly, reflec-
tively for the terrace, his gaze wandering over
the room, to the guitar, the puppet show, the
spot where Maria had stood alone ...

EXT. REAR OF VILLA – NIGHT

The Captain comes out onto the terrace. He
moves to the balustrade, stands looking out
over the lake, his mind filled with thoughts
of Maria ... the CAMERA MOVES UP to
reveal Maria, gazing out into the night from
her bedroom window. Everything about her

attitude and her expression tells us that *she* is filled with thoughts of the Captain.

These scenes were considered too similar to ones that take place later, after Maria's return to the household. Though they were filmed, when Bob previewed the film in Minneapolis he determined that they made the film run too long and were redundant, and he cut them.

People always remark about the beauty of the film, and the locations in and around Salzburg were truly extraordinary. For the scene in the mountain meadow at the beginning of 'Do-Re-Mi' we were on a hillside in Werfen. It was late June, at the end of our location work, and foggy and drizzling when we arrived in the meadow. We couldn't see any mountains, just the soggy slope where we were to have our picnic with Fraulein Maria. We had no idea of the view that surrounded us – until the mist began to lift. It was then that we realized we had been inside a cloud. But even though the clouds above us had dissolved, we still had to wait, because there were clouds beneath us! Bob couldn't film until we could see the valleys below.

While we waited out the weather, we huddled in a barn nearby, practicing songs and telling stories. The air was damp and smelled of fresh-cut hay, but we were warm, wrapped in blankets, and feeling the bond between all of us strengthen. Time just seemed to slow down. Julie and Marc and Saul formed a singing group called the Vocalzones, a name contrived from the throat lozenges that Julie would use to soothe her throat before singing. The high point of their repertoire was 'The Hawaiian War Chant,' and their harmony was inspired by homemade schnapps – the gift of a local farmer.

When the sun finally cleared in that meadow in Werfen, you never saw a film crew work so fast. We filmed Maria leading the children around the meadow like the Pied Piper during the only moment in which that vista had been visible for days.

It was there, on that mountaintop, while we waited for the weather to cooperate, that my 'brothers and sisters' and I filmed *The Grim Reaper* with my eight-millimeter movie camera. I sometimes wonder if it was a subversive reaction to the sentimental movie we were officially making. (Chris Plummer would have appreciated it!) *The Grim Reaper*, a silent film, opens with me examining a hideous-looking hay scythe we'd found in the barn. Later, with a wicked grin, Heather pretends to kill Angela, then me. Our dramatic death throes, which go on and on, were Oscar-worthy performances in our eyes. Unfortunately, the children's tutor then took the scythe away: 'You shouldn't be playing with this! It's too dangerous!' There went our main prop, and the plot of the film sort of falls apart after that. In the next scene, I sneak up behind Bob Wise, who was notorious for being able to take naps anywhere and everywhere. He snores away on camera, blissfully unaware of my presence. *The Grim Reaper* concludes with all seven of us children running down the hillside while Alan Callow, the assistant director's son, mans the camera. As we run down the hill, faster and faster, picking up speed, Kym falls head over heels down the slope. In the film, it looks as if she breaks her neck. This wasn't the only time during shooting when something happened to Kymmie. Fortunately, she survived, unscathed (and unscythed).

Shooting the scenes at the Rocky Riding School, where the Salzburg Music Festival is held in the film, was memorable, if difficult. It was a striking location, but it provided some real challenges, particularly for Ted McCord, the cinematographer. Rather than using a special filter for the nighttime festival scene, we actually filmed at night. The arena is carved out of the side of a cliff and has a hundred archways, each of which had to be lit. Ted and his gaffer rented lights and generators from all over Europe. The catwalk that spanned the auditorium couldn't bear the weight of the spotlight, so Ted constructed an elaborate structure over the audience to support the spot platform.

Fifteen hundred Austrian extras were hired to fill the arena. Our makeup call was at eight-thirty in the evening. Filming went on long into the night, for five nights in row. The extras all had to wear summer clothing, although every night the temperature went down to the thirties. I've often wondered what all those extras thought as they sat through those freezing nights, waiting and waiting for the cameras to roll, then listening to us singing lyrics to our playback recording in a foreign language.

The film crew set out cots for all the children to sleep on, and the younger children would nap in between takes. Kymmie hated being sent to her cot. She hated being the youngest of our group, and always begged to stay up. By the time we were filming the music-festival scenes, she had learned to speak some German, and had also become rather proficient at playing gin rummy. One of her strongest memories of making *The Sound of Music* is playing gin rummy with the 'Nazis' during those long nights at the Rocky Riding School.

Nicky really enjoyed filming the festival scene, because for him it was like being back on stage. The seven of us and Chris and Julie would stand facing those fifteen hundred extras and sing 'Do-Re-Mi' and 'Edelweiss' and 'So Long, Farewell' over and over. But it was so cold. Bottles of brandy and schnapps kept the adult cast and crew going in the early-morning hours as shooting dragged on.

Because of the late hours and the needs of the lighting crew, our Austrian stand-ins (the actors who were our 'doubles') spent a great deal of time with us at the Rocky Riding School. It was during these nights on the set that the other kids and I realized that humor is not universal – at least not when you're trying to translate a pun from English into German.

It began with Kymmie telling elephant jokes. We were trying to break the ice with our Austrian counterparts and so we got a couple of members of the crew who were bilingual to translate the jokes. The young Austrians just looked bewildered when the jokes were translated. Nicky tried one: 'When is a door not a door?' This line was translated, and the Austrian actors waited eagerly for the answer, 'When it's ajar!'

Silence. Translated as 'When it's open,' the punch line didn't have quite the same impact.

Then one of the other kids told the joke about the cannibal who complained that his latest meal hadn't tasted right. He had eaten someone dressed in a burlap sack with a rope tied around his waist. 'Of course,' said the cannibal's friend, 'you shouldn't have stewed him. He was a friar.'

We all laughed, but the Austrians just looked at one another. Our translator explained, 'The translation for them is "he's a brother."'

'Maybe,' I suggested, 'we should hear some typical Austrian jokes so we have a better idea what they like.'

We could tell that the Austrian kids liked that idea. They talked rapidly among themselves, then told a joke. When it was translated for us, it made no sense.

'This is so frustrating!' Kymmie cried. At that moment, she slipped and fell down the stairs that led to the stage, and the seven of us and our Austrian stand-ins burst out laughing. Lesson for the day: slapstick translates.

After we finished the music-festival scenes, we

were back to daytime filming, and shot the scene at the riding school with just the children and Max and Herr Zeller. That was the day when Kymmie was accidentally knocked off the stage by Debbie. The two of them were jockeying for better positions on camera, and Kymmie fell from the stage, hitting the ground so hard she bounced.

Today, Kym and Debbie can laugh about these maneuverings.

'There was definitely a close-up issue,' remembers Debbie.

'I did get more attention than you because I was the youngest,' says Kym. 'But look at what happened when the videotape came out. I'm at the side, so I'm cut out of a lot of scenes.'

'Yeah, yeah, yeah,' says Debbie, grinning. 'Get over it.'

'I just tell everyone to buy the director's cut,' says Kym, grinning right back.

The most dramatic moment during filming was when we almost lost Kym in the lake. She didn't know how to swim. For the scene in which Maria and the children are in the boat, laughing and singing as they approach the Captain and the Baroness on the shore, Bob and the crew had everything choreographed. As Julie fell forward out of the boat into the water, her first job was to grab Kym and carry her to shore. The problem was, when we actually filmed the scene, Julie didn't fall forward – she fell backward out of the boat, and had no idea where Kym was when she surfaced. With the cameras rolling, and Kym going down for the count, Alan Callow jumped into the lake (and the scene) and pulled her out. A home movie taken by Angela's mother catches Alan's rescue on film, as he carries a tearful Kymmie from the lake.

For Kym, the episode was profoundly traumatic. And, of course, we had to reshoot the scene. Hours passed while we all showered and dried our hair, our clothes were washed and dried, and our makeup was reapplied. Then five-year-old Kym Karath had to get back into that boat and get ready to be capsized again. That took courage.

Actually, I don't think any one of us was looking forward to a second dip. Not only was the water cold, but it was also filthy. To top it off, several of the men on the crew teased us that there were leeches in the lake.

But out on the water we went again. This time it would be Heather, not Julie, who would be responsible for grabbing Kym. Men beneath the stern rocked the boat back and forth. We all plunged in. Now Julie fell forward. Heather grabbed Kym, but not before she had ingested more dirty lake water. Bob managed to get enough of the scene on film before Kym threw up on Heather's shoulder. The final cut is a composite of both takes.

Kym never quite overcame her fear of water. 'I never really learned how to swim well,' she admits. 'It just terrifies me. A couple of years ago, my husband put together a montage of photographs from the film as a surprise for me, and there were two shots of us in that boat on the lake. It literally gave me the shakes.'

Alan Callow, the young man who saved Kym, met Kym's older sister Francie (who had also tested for the part of Liesl) when she visited the set, and ended up marrying her. Alan is immortalized on film as the young Nazi who runs onto the stage at the end of the music festival and shouts, 'They're gone!' And Alan's father, assistant director Ridgeway (Reggie) Callow, would himself step out from behind the scenes when the carriage driver of our Austrian fiacre (the horse-drawn carriage used in 'Do-Re-Mi') was unavailable at the last minute. Reggie gamely donned the driver's costume and trotted us down the street.

On the day that Julie filmed her now famous spin in the meadow at the beginning of the movie, we also shot the last scene, in which the Trapp family is hiking over the Alps – so Julie filmed the beginning and ending on the exact same day. Accomplishing this feat took some tricky travel arrangements, for the scenes were shot at locations that were far apart. Julie was taken to Mehlweg, Bavaria, while the rest of us were transported to Obersalzburg-Rossfeld. Julie did the opening shot, which ended up being physically demanding work: the helicopter flying the cameraman blew her off her feet after each take. When that was completed, she was whisked by helicopter to the mountaintop where we all were waiting.

Unfortunately, as soon as Julie arrived, the weather

clouded over. Nonetheless, she changed her costume just in case, and the moment she stepped out of her trailer, the sun came out long enough for us to complete the master shot and subsequent takes (with Chris carrying Kym's double in the more distant shots).

It is ironic that the final scene of the film, when the von Trapps are hiking over the Alps into Switzerland, was filmed only a stone's throw away from Hitler's famed 'Eagle's Nest' at Berchteschgaden. I didn't think much about it when I was twenty-one. I didn't really comprehend what it meant that Hitler's personal haven was right there, just over the hills from Salzburg, or the danger the family faced when they defied the Nazi officials following the Anschluss. But when I think about it now, about walking past Berchteschgaden, it gives me chills. With evil sweeping into their homeland, the von Trapps had made the difficult decision: they would leave Austria.

It was a kind of death. Overnight, they became refugees, with no country, no home. They journeyed to America to find sanctuary, to reinvent themselves, and in the process were reborn. They left behind all that they knew – a city, a community, a house, all their belongings and friends. But, as Maria herself would later say, they were not poor. They just didn't have any money.

The last scene we filmed in Austria was on the St Wolfgang Schafbergbahn Mountain Railway, with all of us waving from the windows of the train. It was one of the few scenes in which Julie's double, Larri Thomas, fills in for her. Since Maria wouldn't be in close-up, Bob could have the second unit shoot us on the train while he continued to work with Julie on the opening scenes in Mehlweg.

Larri is also on screen in the tree-climbing scene, another of the last scenes we shot on location. That day was great fun. It had rained earlier, so the limbs of the trees were damp. The crew hoisted us up into the branches, and we were all swinging high above the ground and laughing. I loved hanging upside down in my tree; it brought out the tomboy in me.

It was a bittersweet day when we rode on the train, since our time in Austria was drawing to a close. All the children's mothers got to be extras in that scene – a nice way to end the many weeks they had spent with us in Salzburg. As usual, the weather was rather gloomy, but this didn't dampen our spirits until the day was over. Then it hit me. Our location filming was complete. We were going home.

The Sound of Music *is a film people like to share with others, as is evident in a story from a golf pro in California.*

'It's always been my favorite movie. I couldn't tell you how many times I've seen it. My best friend in high school and I used to sing to the sound track all the time. We'd sit in my old Mercury Cougar with the eight-track player blaring 'My Favorite Things' and belt out the lyrics as if we were in a karaoke bar.

'Looking back, I realize that The Sound of Music was one of the things that made us become friends. It was uncool to admit to most of my teenage peers how wonderful I thought the movie was, but this one friend shared my love of the film and the music. Our admiration of Music made us know we both valued the same things.

'I now own the video, but before VCRs the only time I could see it was when it was rereleased into theaters. In 1976, when the film was back on the big screen, I called my old friend. We were in our twenties by then, our lives going in different directions, but there was no one else I wanted to see that film with. It was ours. One afternoon, the two of us rendezvoused in our hometown and sat in a theater sharing a tub of popcorn, watching The Sound of Music.

'When the movie ended and the lights came up, the

two of us looked at each other and we both had the same thought at the same time.

' "*You want to stay and see it again?*"

' "*Yeah! Let's!*"

'So we sat for half an hour while the ushers cleaned the theater and a whole new audience trooped in. The lights went down and we watched the whole three hours of Music all over again. It was just as good as the first time.

'I couldn't do that with any other movie – or any other friend. I can't explain it. There is something about that movie that still affects me. It's not just the film itself anymore. It's the memories of watching it, too. Every time I see it, it reminds me of a long afternoon spent with one of the few people in my life who understand me on a deep level.

'The Sound of Music always seems to bring the best parts of me to the surface – just like a lifelong friend.'

THE GAZEBO

We returned from Salzburg with much work still to do. It was July, and we'd been working, sometimes six days a week, without a break since February. Everybody was tired and even a little downcast, as we left behind our magnificent fairy-tale location for the dim sound-stages of Los Angeles.

To make matters worse, I went with my boyfriend Mickey to see the stage version of *The Sound of Music*. After the final curtain, I walked out of the theater completely depressed. I thought it was awful! The story seemed sugary and contrived, and even my favorite musical numbers seemed static on that stage. Maybe it was because I was exhausted from work and travel, but seeing the play convinced me that all our hard work had been for naught. Our film was going to be a dismal flop.

I wasn't the only one feeling low, and Bob Wise sensed the need to lift everyone's spirits. In secret, during our first weeks back in Los Angeles he had William Reynolds (who would later earn an Oscar for editing the film) put together the montage of 'Do-Re-Mi' to screen as a surprise for all of us.

Not only was Bill Reynolds a great editor, so was Bob Wise. He'd cut his teeth inside an editing room, working on films like *The Magnificent Ambersons* and *My Favorite Wife* as well as the masterpiece *Citizen Kane*. One afternoon at the beginning of August, he assembled the cast and crew in the screening room and without any fanfare rolled the film.

What an impact those eleven minutes of film had on us! We sat in the dark, totally enthralled by 'Do-Re-Mi.' It was marvelous. Beautiful. Everyone, even cynical Christopher Plummer, was overwhelmed. And proud! This was the boost we all needed to finish the work at hand. And as we walked out of the screening room, we all knew we were involved in something that was going to be extraordinary. To this day, I can't think of another piece from any other musical that so artfully uses locations to move the story forward. Ernie Lehman had put it on paper, Saul and Marc and Dee Dee had choreographed it, and Bob had put it on film. It was spectacular.

We had many scenes left to shoot, including the arrival of Maria in the von Trapp home, and the party the Captain throws for the Baroness. Chris Plummer, with the help of a retired naval officer, had become quite adept at blowing the bos'n's whistle for the moment when the Captain introduces his children to their new governess. To me, it is in this scene, with all of us marching down the stairs (except for Angela, who wanders in late, reading a book), that it's evident how much taller than me Nicky had become.

Actually, all of the children were growing during the filming. Bob Wise remembers, 'At the outset of the production, we had the children's heights carefully scaled, according to their age in the script. In some cases, this meant giving some of the children lifts in their shoes to make them taller than the other children who were supposed to be younger. But as we began to film, they all started to shoot up, and not necessarily in proportion to each other.'

At first the problem was met by exchanging lifts. After a few weeks, however, Bob found he needed to get daily growth reports in order to make sure newly shot scenes matched what had already been filmed.

'We got hold of a shoemaker in Salzburg,' Bob says, 'and he must have thought we were insane, because we were coming in sometimes twice a week with requests for corrections in the lifts.'

The biggest problem occurred when we returned from Salzburg. Nicky was growing so fast that Bob worried he'd surpass Julie and maybe even Chris. He was certainly taller than me. Using creative camera angles and adding lifts to my shoes (and even a box for me to stand on at one point), Bob was able hide the fact that my 'little brother' had surpassed me in height. But if you look closely at us all lined up, you can see that he had. 'I think they were about to dig a hole for me to stand in,' Nicky jokes now. Today he tops me by a good eight inches.

Nicky's growth spurt also presented a problem for him in scenes where his moves were choreographed. He'd never had much experience with dancing, and his new height made him feel all the more awkward. No matter how hard he tried, he couldn't get his feet to cooperate. For the scene in which Friedrich and Liesl waltz together, Marc and Dee Dee came up with a solution: they had me lead. This gave Nicky footwork to follow, and he looks great in that scene.

One of the most romantic dances ever choreographed followed our little waltz. Chris and Julie's performance of the simple but breathtaking Austrian folk dance, the Laendler, was showstopping. Dee Dee, who has so much incredible work to her credit, from films to television specials to Super Bowl half-time shows, has said that the Laendler is her favorite piece. 'Julie and Chris did us proud. We watch the characters they play fall in love during that dance. Julie hesitating with her hand; the slow spin as they both realize what's happening and the knowledge stops them, holds them suspended – it was marvelous to choreograph, and equally marvelous to watch. Chris was so elegant in that uniform.' Dee Dee grins. 'Even better than in his ballet tights.'

Nicholas Hammond's dancing on camera wasn't over yet. During the filming of 'So Long, Farewell' for the party guests, he was required to do a little spin and a kick. He remembers the moment all too well. 'It was a fourteen-year-old's nightmare, especially with me at such an uncoordinated stage. To make things worse, there were all these extras on hand for that scene, which made me feel like

I was doing it on stage. I love to *act* on stage – but dance? I just remember thinking, Please, dear God, let me get through this without looking like a complete idiot.'

Personally, I think Nicky was terrific in that scene. And I did think the choreography, especially the part that has us on the stairs mimicking a cuckoo clock, was ingenious, and so much fun to film.

Next was the puppet show. The puppets used in the film were made by America's foremost puppeteers, Bil and Cora Baird. Dee Dee Wood, who along with Marc Breaux choreographed the puppet movements on stage, thought the women puppets were too buxom: 'I kept thinking, Should these women puppets be seen on screen? Should children be playing with these?' I never thought much about it myself until recently, when I was watching that scene. Those puppets were pretty well endowed!

I think Julie found the puppet show particularly exhausting. For several days we were in a confined space on a platform high above the puppet stage, and the choreography of the marionettes was intricate. The more complicated moves of those puppets were, of course, done by the Bairds. One day on the set, one of the extras, who didn't know who Bil Baird was, asked him how he managed to get on the picture. And Bil deadpanned, 'Easy. I just pulled a few strings.'

Bil and Cora were marvelous, and patiently

trained Julie and the rest of us to manipulate the puppets. A number of angles show us actually moving the puppets on the stage, and Bil and Cora's work with us made that scene so much more believable and realistic.

At the end of the puppet show, we were supposed to race down off the platform to the Captain and the Baroness and Max. There was a huge step at the bottom of the stage. I was worried about hitting my mark quickly and jumped down hard – and the arches of my feet felt as if they were on fire. I had to race around the corner of the stage smiling and enthusiastic, trying my best not to wince.

The last two scenes we did as an entire family were those in which the Captain sings 'Edelweiss' and 'The Sound of Music' with his children.

When Ernie Lehman first saw the play, he felt the scene in which the Captain first hears his children singing, then joins them in song, was one of the most touching moments he'd ever experienced in theater. 'You know,' he says, 'early on, I took director William Wyler to see that play to try to convince him to direct the film version. As we walked out of the theater he said, "Ernie, I'm sorry, but I hated this show."

'I took him for a midnight walk and I asked him, "You hated the whole thing? What about the moment where the father first sings to the children?"

'Wyler stopped dead in his tracks and looked at me. "You know," he said, "I almost cried right then." He ended up not doing the picture, of course, but I could see by the expression on his face that I was right about that moment, and right about *The Sound of Music*. That scene embodied something universal that would touch the entire world someday if we could capture it on film.'

I loved filming 'Edelweiss' opposite Chris. He was so polished and confident. The subtle way he used his eyes, his small smile at the end, appeared understated to me during rehearsals, but I later saw how powerful these tiny movements became on film. That taught me a lot about acting – the camera records the smallest gesture.

Then it was time to film the last family scene – the scene after the boat has capsized and the children sing 'The Sound of Music' for the Baroness. What I remember most about that day is Nicholas. He stood at attention, his wet hair plastered down on his head, his eyes riveted on Chris, as was called for in the script, but his emotions were real. Nicky was very fond of Chris, and throughout the film he had tried to connect with him, to befriend him. After all, Nicholas loved the stage and had worked on Broadway, and greatly admired Chris as an actor. But Chris was very distant with all the children, including Nicholas.

'For me, that scene is, to this day, very poignant,' Nicky says. 'Here was Christopher Plummer, for whom I had tremendous respect, and the filming was ending, and I still didn't really know him. It was ironic, because what was going on for me

131

during that scene was very real. Our relationship, or lack of relationship, echoed that of Friedrich and the Captain.'

Before we started shooting, Bob Wise told the seven of us, 'This is a song your mother would have taught you, your mother who is now dead. While you sing today, it's not only the experience of your father reconnecting with you emotionally, but the memory of when you used to sit and sing it with your mother.' Bob's direction made filming this scene especially sad, as we all focused on this thought: the only way the Captain would be able to know the words to the song and sing with his children was if they all used to sing it together as a family, before their mother died.

It was a powerful day on the set. Robert Wise actually cried during the final take. And after the scene was completed, Nicky Hammond couldn't hold back his own tears. I don't think Chris had any clue why his young colleague was sobbing in the wings.

It was emotional. That scene marked the end of filming with all the kids. There was a little wrap party just for them. We all sat on the 'So Long, Farewell' steps in the entryway set and drank cider from little champagne glasses. Bob Wise gave each of us a small package with a note. Mine said, 'Dear Charmy, Many thanks . . . for being so convincingly "16"!' Inside the box was a Tiffany key ring with little silver musical notes attached to a pendant inscribed *Charmian Carr. The Sound of Music. 1965.*

We all hugged and said tearful goodbyes that day. If I'd known then how often I'd still see Nicky and Heather and Duane and Angela and Debbie and Kymmie, I wouldn't have felt so sad. In reality, we all should have just said, 'See you soon.'

The film crew moved on to the final stage, the gazebo. This set was beautiful and parklike with its glass-walled gazebo and real sod, all inside a soundstage. Work began with Julie and Chris alone, singing 'Something Good.' It is one of my favorite scenes in the entire film. The song was written specifically for the movie by Richard Rodgers (Oscar Hammerstein had died in 1960), and I thought the music was beautiful.

Ernie Lehman has an axiom: 'Success is being lucky enough to lose the right battles.' In the Broadway play, Rodgers and Hammerstein had a song called 'An Ordinary Couple,' which the Captain and Maria sing as they express their love for each other for the first time. Both Saul and Bob felt the song lacked the romance necessary for that moment in the story, but Ernie balked at the suggestion of eliminating it. He liked 'An Ordinary Couple.' Bob and Saul kept encouraging him to see the scene differently.

'I'm so glad they did,' says Ernie now. 'With "Something Good," the scene ended up being much more moving. For some reason, no matter how many times I've seen it, I always cry during "Something Good." There's something about that scene that gets me right in the heart. And I hate to think that, if I'd clung to "An Ordinary Couple," "Something Good" would never have made it into the film.'

I wasn't there on the days when the scene was filmed, but I heard later what happened: during the shooting, Julie and Chris got a bad case of the giggles.

They were both exhausted. More than half a year on a shoot can do that to you. Julie said it started when one of the huge arc lamps they used to light the scene started making funny noises, not unlike someone making a raspberry off camera. She started laughing and couldn't stop. Laughter can be contagious, even in the most serious professional moments. Pretty soon Chris couldn't stop laughing either.

'Everyone fell on the floor,' he says. 'We never could get through that scene.'

After several botched attempts at putting this romantic and tender moment on film, Bob Wise finally told them both to take a long lunch break to 'walk it off' and come back ready to finish the scene.

By then the pressure to finish the film was intense. Bob was a million dollars over budget and weeks over schedule, and he was well aware of the dire situation Twentieth Century Fox was in. Julie and Chris had been pros throughout the entire production, so Bob was sure the morning was a fluke and that the afternoon shoot would go smoothly. But it didn't work out that way: they lost it again.

Finally, Bob came up with a solution that was brilliant. He decided to shoot their faces partially in shadow, so the camera wouldn't catch their uncontrolled mirth. The two actors drew close together, the light shining between them creating the shape of a heart, and a beautiful moment was born. That's what makes a great director. Rather than be exasperated and lose his temper, Bob Wise used all his creative genius that day to make that scene work, and in the end made it even more memorable.

The very last complete scene filmed for *The Sound of Music* was 'Sixteen Going on Seventeen,' with Rolf and Liesl in the gazebo. It was Dan Truhitte's and my major scene together, and we had spent a lot of time working with Dee Dee and Marc to master the choreography. The dance begins simply, with just hand-holding and backward leans. But as it progresses, the steps become intricate and athletic. We jump up onto the benches of the gazebo, then 'Rolf' leads me through a series of leaps from bench to bench.

I knew the time pressure we were under. Everyone knew. But still Bob maintained his patience. The cinematographer, Ted McCord, had a great deal of trouble getting the scene lit just the way he wanted it. The gazebo was an octagonal structure with real glass on all eight sides, from ground to roof, creating a nightmare for Ted, because light bounced at his lens from eight reflecting surfaces. He couldn't remove the glass, because the scene needed the effect of the raindrops running down the windowpanes. Bob waited patiently until Ted was ready, opting, as always, for perfection rather than speed. Finally, we were ready to shoot.

I changed from my practice shoes into my show shoes, which were exactly the same, except they were brand-new. But unbeknownst to me, the wardrobe department had forgotten to put the rubber skids on the soles of the shoes. Dan and I began the first simple steps. Everything was going fine. But then it happened. I did my first jump up onto a bench with Dan at my side – and I just kept going.

I'd had to hit the bench with power and momentum so I could turn on my toe and jump down again. But since there was no rubber skid to give me any friction or control, I crashed right through the plate-glass panel of the gazebo and landed on the floor of the soundstage, surrounded by shards of glass.

It was a surreal moment. I just lay there on the ground, trying to comprehend what had happened, as everyone around me panicked. I can only imagine what that moment was like for Bob Wise. There he was, under pressure to finish the film with only one scene to go, and I was lying in a pile of glass.

Miraculously, I wasn't badly cut. But when I tried to stand, I realized what the fall had done: my right ankle was severely sprained. As someone ran to fetch the studio doctor, I looked at Bob and silently vowed that I would finish this scene. I wasn't going to let him down.

The doctor gave me a shot for the pain, and a vitamin B_{12} shot (I wasn't quite sure what that was supposed to do). Then they put an ace bandage on my ankle, and a makeup artist actually put makeup on the bandage to try to make it blend in. Finally, they had me put on a pair of dark-tan nylons, and we continued.

If you freeze-frame a video of that dance and look closely at my right ankle, you can see that it looks slightly paler and thicker than the left. That is the ace bandage, almost perfectly camouflaged. My ankle hurt, but it didn't fail me on my kicks and turns. I knew that dance so well I could do it in my sleep. I never let it enter my head that I wouldn't finish the scene. After all, dancing was the one real talent I'd had when they hired me. I'd waited seven months for my chance to perform 'Sixteen Going on Seventeen' – my big scene! The only alternative would have been to cut the dancing from the scene or have a stunt double do my part. There's no way I would have considered either of those options. If I'd broken my leg in three places and had a hundred stitches on my face, I was going to do that dance.

It took several hours to get all the angles. At the end of that day, I had one of the most thrilling moments of my life. All the union technicians, the electrical riggers and grips and propmen and boom handlers and gofers, gave me a standing ovation. I had never seen them do that before on the set, and I felt so honored and proud. We'd done it!

At the end of the gazebo dance, after Liesl receives her first kiss from Rolf, she spins out into the rain, arms stretched wide, and gives a squeal of joy. I had begun the film soaking wet, and it seemed only appropriate that I would end it soaking wet, too.

That day marked the end of principal filming on *The Sound of Music*. I had been there on Soundstage 15 at the very beginning when the cameras rolled, and I was there on the same stage when the film was put to bed. It was natural for me to asume that my role as Liesl von Trapp had ended. I would soon learn, however, that my association with her was, in fact, only beginning.

I'm often amazed at how the film leaves a lifelong impression on individuals. I love this story from a woman in New England.

'I was born in 1965, the year the film was released, and The Sound of Music has always been my favorite movie. I could probably recite the whole thing. I watch it about twenty times a year. I love the story, and the film brings back so many wonderful memories of my childhood.

'I have the most wonderful father in the world. He is, at six foot nine, the largest teddy bear on the face of the earth. He would do anything for anybody.

'When I was small, we would go to a park near our house that had a gazebo. It was very similar to the one in the movie, with benches circling the inside. And my favorite thing to do as a child was to pretend I was Liesl. I would run along each bench, and my dad would help me leap to the next one. That is one of my strongest childhood memories, having this big bear of a man I adored helping me soar from bench to bench.

'My daughter was pretty much encouraged to have The Sound of Music as her favorite film, too, because I watch it so often. I won her over. And what was strange was, she began to do the same thing. I never told her about my leaping from bench to bench. But one day, we walked to the gazebo, and she knew just what to do.

139

'So the film has become a part of my life. Whenever I'm in the car, humming a song, it ends up being one from The Sound of Music. My daughter and I are always serenading each other with 'How Do You Solve a Problem Like Maria.' And my son, who's only two and a half, is always asking to watch the video.

'My daughter isn't as choosy as I was when I'd pretend to be Liesl, dancing around the gazebo. She'll let anyone help her leap from bench to bench. But I never let anyone play in the gazebo with me but my dad. To me, he's the best dad who ever lived – and that's our dance.'

DARLEEN

As Kurt hits his high note in 'So Long, Farewell,' grinning at his father as he prances off to bed, listen closely to his voice. That is my little sister, Darleen.

Darleen was born with a gift. She got the music gene. A child prodigy with perfect pitch, she could listen to a song once and have it tonally memorized. Hers is an intuitive genius, not technical, and her voice, from the time she was a very small child, has been unique and beautiful.

Irwin Kostal, the music director for *The Sound of Music*, was desperate for children with fine singing voices to enhance the other children's voices on the sound track.

Darleen was thirteen when she auditioned for Saul and Irwin. They listened to her sing just one song and went crazy over her voice. In fact, they felt she was so good, they gave her a screen test, even though the parts for the other children were already cast. Like me, however, Darleen had never acted professionally, so ultimately she was hired, along with three other children, just to sing on the sound track.

Since Darleen put in six weeks of work on the picture, even though her face is never on the screen, she became eligible for residuals. Every time *The Sound of Music* is shown on television, we each receive a check from the studio for the exact same amount. The most recent one was for $37.42.

When the von Trapp children sing 'The Sound of Music' listlessly for the Baroness – the scene on the terrace when we gradually stop singing – it is the only time on the entire sound track that the children's voices are not enhanced by the additional singers. Yet even in that song Darleen's voice is present, singing not the melody along with the children but the high notes that counter it.

Like me, Darleen began her career with *The Sound of Music*. Unlike me, Darleen continued acting in film and television from that moment forward. It began one day on the Fox backlot.

Like all the other minors involved in the film, Darleen, by regulation, attended the studio school for three hours every day. As she was walking back to school from the studio commissary after lunch, a writer stopped her. 'Excuse me!' he called. 'Are you an actress?'

'No,' Darleen replied, going on to explain that she was a singer, doing a voice dub on a sound track.

That didn't seem to faze the writer at all. 'Would you be interested in reading for a TV show I'm writing?' And that is how Darleen Carr's acting career began.

The writer was working on a Canadian television series called 'The Littlest Hobo,' a show like 'Rin-Tin-Tin' that starred a dog, and so, after Darleen finished her work on the sound track, she flew to

Canada and made her acting debut in a segment of the program. The producers were so pleased with her performance that they commissioned a script for a full-length film for her (and the dog), and the following winter Darleen spent more than a month in Canada shooting the feature *The Littlest Hobo*.

That led to a television stint on a program called 'The John Forsythe Show.' And that led to Walt Disney.

Walt Disney was looking for the next Hayley Mills, and he thought he'd found her in my little sister. Darleen had a forty-five-minute interview with him, alone in his office, singing and playing her guitar. By the time she walked out the door, she had been signed to a long-term contract.

Her first project for Disney was as the voice of the little princess in the animated film *The Jungle Book*. Thereafter, Disney involved her in everything from the two-hour television movie *Gallagher Goes West* for 'The Wonderful World of Disney,' to special performances at Disneyland, to voice dubbing, and then to a Disney feature with Dean Jones and Maurice Chevalier called *Monkeys, Go Home*. She got to record two songs with Monsieur Chevalier, who was by then rather old and on occasion missed beats of the music. He would smile that inimitable smile of his and say to the director, 'Don't worry. I will jest look at zee kid and she will show me when to sing.'

Darleen was on the Disney lot nonstop, and was amazed to discover that every single day Walt

Disney visited every single set. He knew each person by name, from the directors and the actors to the custodians and the accountants. His death in December of 1966 not only shocked everybody, but it threw the studio into absolute turmoil. Eventually, Darleen's contract was dropped. She was, in hindsight, grateful to be let go, for it allowed her to take on a variety of different roles and develop into a young actress rather than a child star. She did a lot of television, including a long-term role as Karl Malden's daughter on 'The Streets of San Francisco.' She hasn't stopped working since.

Her acting career gave Darleen the early independence she sorely needed. Since she was very young, she'd dealt with our parents' problems daily. One night when we were still living in Chicago, our parents were having a fight in the kitchen and tiny Darleen walked in, placed herself between them, and solemnly declared, 'I want to die.' That stopped them in their tracks.

Darleen was only six when Dad and Mom separated. Mom always said that Darleen was Dad's favorite because she was such a tomboy. He loved that she liked to do things outdoors. After our parents split up, Dad still took Darleen horseback riding. One day, he was picking her up, and came up the steps to our house as Darleen came out the door, Mom behind her. Mom saw Dad's girlfriend waiting in the car and went crazy. Screaming and yelling at him, she slapped Dad over and over in the face while Darleen kept crying out, 'Don't hit my daddy!'

Dad was wearing a pair of sunglasses, and when Mom hit him, he was cut below his eye. He still took Darleen riding that day, but it was the last time any of us would see him for years. He simply never came back. There was a phone conversation in which he explained that he felt the damage of that event was more harmful to us than his just staying away. And that was that.

It was as if our father had died. And since he was no longer around to defend himself, or even remind us what he was like, he became an easier target for Mom to attack. Her messages were clear and relentless: Our father was a horrible man. He had never supported us. He wasn't faithful. He was a miserable human being, and a total failure. She repeated these things over and over, like a mantra.

When Darleen was eight years old, she put a note in her jewelry box that said, 'I never want to get married. Ever.' Mom found the note, and she was so proud! To her, it meant that she was succeeding – Darleen was learning her lessons that men were untrustworthy and unnecessary. Mom actually saved that note. She kept it in her wallet as you would a favorite picture.

But Darleen missed Dad – we all did. He was the one who would take her to do her most favorite thing in the world: horseback riding. She was the most horse-crazy kid ever born. She didn't just pretend to ride horses when she was little – she actually would pretend she *was* a horse. She'd walk around on all fours, rearing back and whinnying. When she began to earn money from acting, there was only one thing she wanted to buy: her own horse.

Her love of horses and riding continued as she grew older. In 1991, she was working with a horse on a lunge rope, putting it through its paces, when all of a sudden the horse balked and then charged past her, kicking her once in the chest.

The kick broke all the bones in her sternum and stopped Darleen's heart. The doctors later said it was a traumatic heart attack. She was clinically dead. For three minutes, Darleen was gone from us, although I wouldn't know this until later that day, after they had brought her back and she was safe and recuperating in intensive care. The only thing she remembers is that she felt peaceful and could hear voices, as if from far away, calling to her.

The day we almost lost Darleen, I realized how important both of my sisters are to me. We are so different from one another, and Darleen especially seems like my opposite at times. She is volatile where I am passive, strong where I am vulnerable. But, dissimilar as we may be, we are a matched set. We each have our own issues and fears, but our combined qualities make us invincible. We are a family.

Listen closely to the children's voices in *The Sound of Music*. When you hear those high notes – that is my little sister, Darleen. Passionate and gifted, she is one of the high notes in my life.

*T*he powerful Rodgers and Hammerstein score has affected generations, as evidenced in this woman's story.

'My mother had a brain tumor removed when I was only five. She couldn't say a word for six months, and then she couldn't speak well. On those rare occasions when I brought friends home, I would tell them my mother was from a foreign country to explain the funny way she talked. There was frequent tension in our house. My parents would argue.

'I was taken to see The Sound of Music for my seventh birthday. It was an evening show all the way out (a twenty-minute drive!) in Providence, Rhode Island, THE CAPITAL. It was a momentous and special night when our whole family was together, and it has always remained with me. The movie comforted me. It represented all generations: the old nuns, the middle-aged couples, the young adults, the children – and the children were cared for.

'I was given the album when I was nine. I listened to it for days and days. The music is so special to me. It became a part of my life, of who I am.

'So, when my son Spencer reached the age of watching videos, he received The Sound of Music to balance The Lion King and Dumbo. He was riveted. He especially loved the children singing. Shortly after his introduction to the film at age three, he really took off as a boy: running, falling, crying, having scary dreams, getting time-outs. I had always sung soothing songs to him as I held him, but it was when I tried "My Favorite Things" that he really calmed down. It is magical.

'His teacher told me that one day at school; Spencer was playing alone, putting toys away, and she heard him singing. "Raindrops on roses an' whiskers on kittens . . ." He sang the song all the way through.

'It means a great deal to me that these special songs from my childhood are now a part of my son's life. It's a part of his heritage – because it's a part of me.'

THE PREMIERE

Nicky and Heather and Duane and Angela and Debbie and Kymmie and I arrived at the Fox Wilshire Theater in a fiacre, an Austrian horse-drawn carriage just like the one we had used in 'Do-Re-Mi.' It was March 10, 1965. We had spent the entire day at the studio getting ready for the premiere, dressing in our costumes from the party scene, being prepped on all that would happen that evening. It had been half a year since we'd all been together, and it was so good to see everybody.

The premiere of *The Sound of Music* was an event that took place at the end of the golden era of Hollywood. All the major Hollywood stars attended, dressed to the nines. Floodlights filled the night sky and a red carpet led from the street across the sidewalk, up the steps, and through the doors of the theater. As our carriage pulled up in front, a sea of people awaited us. The seven of us climbed down and were immediately overwhelmed by the roar of the crowd, the flashing of cameras, the applause, as we followed Julie and Chris (who had arrived before us by limousine) up the red carpet. Inside were hundreds more people, film and television stars and the press and special guests, and it all became a whirl.

Heather remembers that Christopher Plummer

came over to her, a cigarette in his hand, put his arms around her as if she were a long-lost friend, and said, 'Heather! It's been so long since I last saw you!' She couldn't recall his ever speaking to her before, in all the months of rehearsals and filming, and suddenly here he was, her best pal. All Heather could think of was, 'Oh my god. He's talking to *me*.' Cameras flashed to record his embrace of her, and then Chris disappeared into the crowd.

Lorne Greene of 'Bonanza' was the master of ceremonies, along with Army Archerd. The event was sponsored by the American Cancer Society, so he said a few words about the charity the premiere would support and then introduced all of us. We stood there, smiling, stunned by all the flashbulbs, recognizing so many people in the crowd: Fred Astaire, Groucho Marx, Dorothy Malone, Polly Bergen, Zsa Zsa Gabor, Raquel Welch, Frank Sinatra, James Garner, Phil Silvers, Yvette Mimieux, Rod Taylor, Kirk Douglas, Agnes Moorehead, Jerry Lewis, and Sharon's and my childhood idol, Doris Day.

My sister Darleen, busy working as an actress, didn't attend, but Mickey Levey was waiting in the lobby for me, as were Sharon and her date. We milled around, stargazing and gawking, until finally it was time to move into the theater and take our seats.

The Sound of Music was what was called a 'road show' in the sixties. It was edited to be seen like a Broadway play, with an overture and an inter-mission and, for its initial release, reserved seats. The premiere was the first time I would ever see the entire picture. I had seen the first eight rolls at a small studio screening. That was a thrill, especially because I sat with Richard Rodgers and his wife. They were so sweet to me, so encouraging, and so impressed with the film. Now, along with some of the biggest stars in Hollywood, I was seeing all two hours and fifty-two minutes. I had very high expectations based on what I had already seen – and I wasn't disappointed.

It was strange to sit there and watch myself on a huge screen. I had heard so many actresses say they couldn't stand to see how they looked in their films. I had the opposite reaction – I thought I looked great! It was exhilarating to see the com-plete movie – as well as to find myself seated in front of Gregory Peck. I was dying to introduce myself to him, but during the intermission, the studio people whisked us all away for more photo-graphs, so I never got the chance to shake his hand.

After the film was over, a private party followed at the legendary Chasen's restaurant. Everyone affiliated with the film was there: Bob and Ernie and Chris and Julie and Saul and all the children. It was such an exciting night, packed with emotions. I can't remember what we ate or what we said – but I can remember exactly how it *felt:* it was as if I was inside an enchanted fairy tale, living in a dream. I wished that night could go on forever.

One of the most enthusiastic early reviews of *The Sound of Music* came from Maria von Trapp herself. Bob had arranged a special screening for Maria and her personal guests in New York in late February, just before the world premiere. Maria immediately wrote him a thank-you note.

Dear Robert Wise:
You are a much greater artist than I could ever have thought. You have no idea how worried and how indescribably happy I am now after reliving that portion of my life which you have so masterfully recreated. In the name of my family and myself I thank you.

Your friend,
Maria von Trapp

The reviews following the Los Angeles premiere were equally wonderful and positive, giving Bob and Saul and Ernie and the producers at Fox an opportunity to breathe a sigh of relief. The world premiere of the film – which had taken place eight days earlier, on March 2, in New York City – had left them shaken. I hadn't attended, but Julie and Chris were flown in by Fox, and Bob Wise and Darryl Zanuck had been there. They awoke the morning after the premiere to brutal reviews.

... One star and much scenery do not a two-hour-and-fifty-minutes-plus-intermission entertainment make ... This last, most remunerative

156

and least inspired, let alone sophisticated, of the Rodgers and Hammerstein collaborations is square and solid sugar. Calorie-counters, diabetics, and grown-ups from eight to eighty best beware . . . The movie is for the five to seven set and their mommies who think their kids aren't up to the stinging sophistication and biting wit of *Mary Poppins* . . .

Judith Crist
New York Herald Tribune
March 3, 1965

The New York reviews of *The Sound of Music* were painfully negative and mean-spirited. Bob Wise, Darryl Zanuck, Saul Chaplin, and Ernie Lehman were shocked and hurt. As Ernie says, 'Those first reviews were hard to take – but only for a while.'

Bob and Saul held on to one ray of hope. They still believed they had a hit on their hands, because the people of Minneapolis and Tulsa had told them they did. Bob had screened a single sneak preview in each of those two Midwestern cities at the end of January, and the response cards were phenomenal. Ninety-nine percent of the viewers gave *The Sound of Music* the highest possible marks. So Bob Wise didn't panic when he read Judith Crist's review the morning after the film premiered in New York. He was still sure he had a winner. He would soon be proved right.

Other critics and audiences loved the film, pure and simple. The response began slowly at first, but within weeks, it was evident that something extraordinary was happening. From coast to coast, audiences were turning out in record numbers to see the film – and then coming back again and again. In some cities, like Salt Lake City and Orlando and Albany, the number of people attending the film exceeded the entire populations of those cities in a matter of just a few months – and the film was playing only on a *single* theater screen. Repeat audiences would cause the profits to soar and critics to rename the film 'The Sound of Money.'

I believe it's safe to suggest that without *The Sound of Music* there would be no Twentieth Century Fox. The film didn't just rescue the studio from the brink of financial ruin, it helped bankroll films for the next twenty years. Between 1966 and 1972, it was the all-time highest-grossing film, and if adjusted for inflation today, would probably still surpass the profits of almost any other movie. *The Sound of Music* would remain in its initial general release for an unprecedented fifty-seven months – nearly five years. Even blockbusters like *Titanic* have not surpassed that mark.

The film wasn't the only moneymaker. The sound track sold more than one million copies in the first month it was released! To this day, it still sells and sells. It is the most successful sound track of all time – which made many people assume that those of us involved were made rich beyond our wildest dreams. The truth is, except for Julie, no one who sang on the sound track ever received a penny from it. And we certainly didn't share in any of the profits from the film.

I always say *The Sound of Music* made me wealthy spiritually. I absolutely believe that. Would I have preferred having a 'piece of the action'? Absolutely. Though I made good money and I wasn't the one taking the financial risk on the film, the movie has made hundreds of millions of dollars so far, and seems destined to go on forever. It would have been a generous gesture for the studio to distribute bonuses to everyone, but studios are not historically known for such benevolence.

In January of 1966, Wise and Zanuck and Chaplin exacted their revenge on the critics who had lambasted their film when *The Sound of Music* won the Golden Globe Award for Best Picture and Julie Andrews won for Best Actress. I got to accept Bob's statuette on his behalf. The film went on to win awards everywhere, being named Best Foreign Film in Peru, Italy, and Japan, and receiving top honors as the Best Family Film from the Federation of Motion Pictures Council. Then, on April 18, 1966, *The Sound of Music* earned five Academy Awards (out of ten nominations), including a Best Director Oscar for Robert Wise, and surpassing *Doctor Zhivago* to win the Oscar for Best Picture of the Year.

Saul wrote about what it was like to arrive at the Academy Awards with Julie. 'As we neared the auditorium . . . I got out first, then helped

159

Julie out. There was such an ear-shattering screech from the fans the moment they saw her that I was literally stunned motionless. I don't believe I've ever heard a more terrifying sound in my life. Julie, accustomed to this kind of reception and ever gracious, smiled through it all as we walked into the theater.'

Bob Wise was unable to attend because he was filming *The Sand Pebbles* in Hong Kong. Julie accepted his Oscar for Best Director. Then Saul sat waiting in the audience, getting ready to feign his forced gracious-loser smile, when Jack Lemmon announced that *The Sound of Music* was the Best Picture of the Year. Saul accepted, saying, 'If Bob Wise were here, I'm sure he'd thank everyone connected with the picture and the Academy membership for voting him this Award. Instead, I'm going to take this opportunity to thank him for making the filming of *The Sound of Music* such a rewarding and stimulating experience.' Saul's words echoed my own feelings. Bob had directed the film with such patience, and such vision, and I was so grateful to have been a part of it.

On the gunboat where he was filming in Hong Kong, everything broke into pandemonium when the Best Picture Oscar was announced. Firecrackers went off, and Chinese dragon dancers that the crew had secreted in the hold came charging out, banging drums.

One of the first things Bob did was to send Ernest Lehman a telegram.

DEAR ERNIE YOU OWN A GIANT SHARE
OF ALL WE WON MONDAY NIGHT.
MANY MANY THANKS. BOB   APR 21 66

It was a nod to all of Ernie's efforts to make sure *The Sound of Music* made it onto film, and also Bob's way of congratulating Ernie for the job he'd done on the script. Everyone was shocked that Ernie hadn't even been nominated for best screenplay.

I wasn't at the Oscars that night. I was in the Caribbean, working for Fox, promoting the film. I was so excited when I heard the results, but I also remember being disappointed that *Doctor Zhivago* had won so many. 'We only won five?' I said, incredulous upon hearing the news. 'We deserved all ten!' Of course, those awards were only the beginning. No one imagined how successful the picture would become.

But on that night back in March 1965, the night of the Los Angeles premiere, after I got home and the excitement had died down, I was exhausted and fell into bed. I don't know what I dreamed that night, but I know I could never have conceived in my wildest dreams that *The Sound of Music* would inspire repeat audiences for generation after generation. The wave of enthusiasm began slowly, but before long, it reached tidal proportions, worldwide.

'*My grandmother Maria von Trapp died when I was fifteen. She was a great story-teller, but she never talked about* The Sound of Music. *She never led me to believe there was anything important about the film.*

'*I saw the movie when I was very young, too young to remember. My parents tell me that I cried at the end. But as I got older, I held the film at arm's length. In fact, I made it a point not to watch the film. I guess by not watching it I was trying to prevent the movie from taking over my life. People would treat me like I was a celebrity because I was a von Trapp, and that made me uncomfortable. So, when people would ask me things like, "Is is true that the nuns stole the spark plugs?," I could answer, "I don't have any idea what you're even talking about. I never watch that movie." I think that's in part why I became competitive in skiing – I wanted an identity that was separate from these famous, but partially fictitious, film von Trapps.*

'*I didn't see the movie again until I was in my twenties. I was in Mexico, studying Spanish, and with the encouragement of my host family, I went with them and watched the film in subtitles. I could justify to myself going to see it because it was for an academic reason. But as I watched it, I realized how powerful* The Sound of Music *is – the story, the landscape, and especially the music by Rodgers and Hammerstein.*

I'll always be grateful to my host family for motivating me to go.

'It was on that day that I learned the Spanish verb extrañar, *which means to miss a person emotionally. The children use it when Maria leaves, and it stuck with me that day, and has ever since. I was five thousand miles from home, and missed my parents and my family.* Extrañar.

'At our core, we von Trapps are very passionate, very emotional. That Spanish verb made me think about my father's brothers and sisters and parents, and how difficult leaving their home and friends and country must have been. For such deep-feeling people, it could not have been easy to make that choice.

'I'm glad my grandmother wrote books about her experiences, but I wish I could talk to her about them in person. I have so many questions now. What was it really like coming into the family, becoming the stepmother to seven children? When I'm teaching children on the ski slope, and I have a big group, I think about her sometimes. How did she handle it?

'When it's summer in the States, I head to the ski resort in Portillo, Chile, where I teach skiing in the Andes Mountains. This annual pilgrimage has taught me about the worldwide impact of* The Sound of Music. *Children from all over South America come up to me. They are so beautiful, as they look up at me with their big eyes and ask, "¿Es verdad que tu eres el nieto de la novicia rebelde?" That was the title of the film:* La Novicia Rebelde. *These children want to know, am I really the grandson of the rebellious novice?*

163

'My grandmother was a great storyteller. My father inherited that gift from her, and I hope I have inherited it from him. There are many stories that are a part of my family heritage, but the story of The Sound of Music is the one that will always define my family to others. I can embrace it now. I smile at these little children and say, "Sí." I am the grandson of the rebellious novice. I am proud of that story. It is based upon my family – but it truly belongs to everyone.'

—Sam von Trapp

THE AMBASSADOR

I wouldn't understand for months. It was just a movie, after all. Not until I'd traveled around the world and witnessed the outpouring of emotion and enthusiasm in dozens of countries and cities would I begin to comprehend the impact *The Sound of Music* was having on audiences around the globe.

Most films open in general release in a thousand theaters across the country. But in the mid-sixties, there was a trend toward opening big films on a small number of screens. So, in March of 1965, *The Sound of Music* opened in the United States in only 131 theaters, each equipped with seventy-millimeter screens and six-track stereophonic sound.

Since Twentieth Century Fox had signed me to a seven-year contract, they turned me into an ambassador for the film. I traveled alone, appearing at premieres and special events across the country and, later, around the world. It wasn't unheard-of for an actor to do this for a month or so, but I was on the road for almost two whole years. Though it had long been my dream to travel, this was more than I'd ever wished for! Fox began by sending me on domestic trips to: Chicago. Atlanta. Kansas City. Miami. Indianapolis. Milwaukee. Cleveland. Buffalo. Dallas. Seattle. And then they sent me across oceans. To the capitals of Europe. Asia. Central America. The Far East. And, ultimately, Australia. I've promoted the film on every continent except Antarctica.

The Sound of Music broke box-office records around the world. It was one of the first musicals dubbed in other languages, with the entire sound track translated. Saul Chaplin deserves the lion's share of the credit for the film's success in other parts of the world. He meticulously oversaw the musical translations in every country, and the overwhelming response of foreign audiences is a testament to the efforts he made to have the film – and the music – speak to people in their own language. I would love to know how some of the lyrics translated. The various titles by which the film is known around the globe certainly aren't verbatim. For example, in Germany, *The Sound of Music* is called *My Song, My Dream*. In Egypt, it's *Love and Tenderness*. In Thailand, *Charms of the Heaven Sound*. And in Hong Kong, it is called *Fairy Music Blow Fragrant Place, Place Here*.

In Mexico, the film is *La Novicia Rebelde – The Rebellious Novice*. The studio sent me to Mexico City to attend the premiere, and I was taken to a bullfight. I was sitting in a VIP box at the edge of the ring, and before the fight began the matador came over. Swirling his cape and staring at me, he bowed deeply and said something in Spanish.

'He has dedicated the bull to you,' my escort whispered in my ear.

'Oh,' I said, trying to appear grateful. I love animals, and the last thing I wanted was to have this man kill a bull on my behalf. I could barely watch the fight. When the bull was being prodded with long poles to anger and provoke him, I had to turn away. Next the matador stabbed the bull with three short spears, and then, as he turned toward me and bowed, the bull charged. The matador turned – too late. The bull knocked him to the ground and ran over him. I was torn between my concern for the matador and my desire to cheer the bull.

Later, I visited the bullfighter at the hospital and took him a medallion as a gift from the studio. I was told he would be back on his feet soon, and of course I was glad. But I always wondered what happened to that bull. Technically, he had 'won' the fight. I like to think he survived.

I met up with Nicky and Heather and Duane and Angela and Debbie and Kymmie in New York to promote *The Sound of Music* on 'The Ed Sullivan Show.' We were all wearing our 'So Long, Farewell' costumes from the film as Mr Sullivan introduced us. He was just as stiff and awkward in person as he appeared on screen. For a man who stood in front of huge audiences every week, he seemed very shy.

I'd made television appearances before, but never in front of an audience of the size we faced that night. We stood on the stage before cameras that projected our image to millions of people who watched the 'big shoo' every Sunday night. The seven of us lip-synched 'So Long, Farewell' to the film-score playback. Lots of performers do this – even in Broadway plays – to ensure that the audience hears a perfect rendition. I didn't feel nervous. I've always found that, once I'm on stage, something takes over and the nervousness disappears and I just perform. But I have to admit, it hit me that night with Ed Sullivan how big the film was becoming, and how much my life had changed. Little more than a year earlier, I'd been testing urine samples in a doctor's office. Now I was singing to people, coast to coast.

And it wasn't just in America. Now I jetted to the far corners of the earth. I didn't get to sightsee much, because I was always working, but my passport quickly filled up with stamps. People told me I was a natural traveler. I loved flying. I actually loved turbulence. On one flight, even the stewardesses became airsick, yet the bumpier it got the more I enjoyed it.

Everywhere I went, I was treated like royalty, put up in the presidential suites at hotels, and ferried to and from airports and appointments by limousine. My schedule was rigorous. In many ways, promoting the film was harder than making it. Sometimes I'd be in two foreign countries or several cities in a single day. In each country I visited, the routine was the same. A Twentieth Century Fox representative would meet me at the airport or train station. There would be a long list of appointments, everything from interviews to meetings with local dignitaries as well as introducing the film at theaters. We'd arrive at a cinema for a premiere or a special showing, I would say a few words, and the movie would start.

People ask me how many times I've seen *The Sound of Music*. I know the exact number: nine. But I can't say how many times I've seen the beginning: Hundreds. Maybe more than a thousand. At each event I'd sit and watch the first scenes of the mountains of Austria with birds chirping in the background, the music building, the aerial camera angling down over the mountain to the meadow, closer and closer, until Julie Andrews came into view. Then, as Julie did her spin, I'd quietly slip out the door. I've always been grateful to Bob and everyone else responsible that the film is so beautiful. I've never minded watching that opening scene. Still, I don't think I could sit through the whole movie as many times as some people have.

January 6, 1966, was a typical day on the promotional tour. I began the day in Wales. I took the train to Scotland, where I visited Glasgow, then Edinburgh. In each city there was a series of events: two press receptions, two television interviews, one radio interview. In the morning, I attended a private reception with the lord provost of Glasgow; in the evening, I appeared at the screening in Edinburgh. The next morning, when I departed, 'Sixteen Going on Seventeen' was blaring from the public-address system at the train station. On January 7, I was in Newcastle for three newspaper interviews, two radio shows, and so on. And on.

Generally, everything went smoothly, though at one premiere, when I was wearing a beautiful cream-colored satin gown, a waiter spilled gravy all over my dress. Later, I had to go up and speak in front of everyone looking as if I was eating-impaired.

Promoting the film for months and months did get tiring. Twentieth Century Fox put together a scrapbook for me of all the print coverage of my tour. Some newspaper articles reveal the days when all the touring was beginning to wear me down.

'Sometimes (when reviewing my good luck) I can't believe it. And sometimes, I wish it hadn't happened.'

'I'm getting a little tired now . . .'

'Do I get bored? Of course I do! Everywhere I go I have to answer the same questions. The only saving grace is that it is always different people who are asking the questions.'

Other interviews reveal my youthful hopes for the future:

'I know what I want to do. I don't want to be a sexy bombshell. I want to play parts that all people will love. I don't like to go to a depressing movie, so why should I play depressing parts?'

★ ★ ★

> *'What I really want to do is get married and have a family.'*

Overall, being an ambassador was great fun, and I adored the travel. I went to several cities in Germany. The studio invested a lot of money promoting the film there, but it did not do well, perhaps because the war was still such a recent memory. The German distributor for Fox took matters into his own hands. Without any permission from the studio, he simply cut out the third act of the film and slapped the closing credits back on. If you had seen the film in Germany, it would have ended with Maria's marriage to the Captain. German audiences never saw the Nazis marching into the town plaza or the von Trapps fleeing over the Alps. It was revisionist history, in the guise of a business decision. Of course, the studio (not to mention Bob and Saul) was furious. The manager was fired and the film was restored – and German audiences stopped coming.

Despite the poor box-office numbers, everywhere I went in Germany I was met by enthusiastic fans. I traveled the entire country, from Düsseldorf to Cologne and Munich, and never encountered any protest. Still, Germany remains to this day one of the only countries in the entire world where the film was not a commercial success.

Many Germans argued that the problem was that *The Sound of Music* was a remake. *Die Trapp Familie*, made in Germany in 1956, the very first dramatization of Maria von Trapp's story, was the most successful German film made in the fifties. It inspired the musical on Broadway, which was later transformed into the film we made. I have had Germans say to me, 'We had already seen the story and didn't understand why the Americans felt the need to redo it. The German version was a big hit.'

But *Die Trapp Familie* does not tell exactly the same story as *The Sound of Music*. In the scene following Maria's wedding to the Captain, she has her first child. Then the family meets Father Wasner, the priest who helped them become a singing group. The German film focuses more on the von Trapps' traveling to America, their struggle to become established entertainers, and their ultimate triumph as the Trapp Family Singers. It does not emphasize why they left Austria.

One thing that surprises many Americans is that the film positively flopped in Austria. *The Sound of Music* played in Salzburg's theaters for only three days, after which it was pulled because of poor attendance. Although the Austrians had been very supportive of us during our work on location, they felt that the film confused locales and took too much dramatic license with the von Trapps' story.

But, the dismal response of these two countries aside, *The Sound of Music* broke attendance records in almost every other part of the world. And letters addressed to me in care of Twentieth Century

Fox began to arrive within a week of the film's premiere. They came from people of all ages, from all over the world. From Asia to Australia, from Beirut to Bombay, fans young and old wrote to share with me how much *The Sound of Music* meant to them. Couples wrote to tell me they'd named their child Liesl after my character, and hundreds of children wrote to tell me of their aspirations to become actors after seeing the film. Many young men wrote me love letters. One, a sailor off the coast of South Africa, sent ten pages in which he described the beauty of the ocean and told me that all men at sea think of a girl in a faraway place – and he always thought of me. Another, in Manila, very nearly proposed marriage.

I was delighted to hear from one of my old teachers back in Chicago, Sister Mary Florence, who'd attended a screening of *Music* along with eight hundred other nuns. She wrote to let me know she felt I'd done all right 'music-wise': she'd tried in vain to teach me piano in the second grade.

Portraying Liesl gave me an opportunity to touch so many people, even people from my own past. What a gift! It was – and continues to be – such an incredible experience to hear from so many people. I still receive many such letters, decades after the film's release.

But there was a negative aspect to all this recognition. As the popularity of the film grew, I was exposed to what it meant to be a 'studio property.' It was part of being an actor back then, and I'm sure such practices still exist today. Fans clamor for personal information about their favorite actors. The studio publicity department complies – in the way they see fit.

To make me more interesting to people, the Fox publicists exaggerated certain things about me. They even released outright fabrications. The one that bothered me most was the story that I had lied about my age. I don't know when or how it got started. But I never lied to anyone about how old I was when I interviewed for the part of Liesl. Why would I? They always knew I was twenty-one. Bob's and Saul's notes made on a casting sheet from my interview for the part acknowledge my age and their concern about it.

But the fact that I wasn't sixteen was something the studio became quite obsessed with keeping from the public. Apparently, they felt my real age would turn people off and affect profits. I don't know why. Everywhere I went, the Fox press releases preceded me, and they always made me out to be three or four years younger than I was. I was instructed to go along with this fabrication: 'Don't tell anyone your real age.'

'All right,' I said. 'But I won't lie.' I had to be somewhat cagey in responding to questions about my age.

One reporter from Canada asked me, 'It says here that you're eighteen, but that's not right, is it?'

By then I was actually twenty-three, so I grinned

at him and said, 'You know, they keep changing my age, so that I can hardly remember how old I am.'

'What's the big deal about your age?'

'I don't know. I think it's all silly. I don't know why they don't tell the truth.'

'So how old are you?'

'I'm really not supposed to say.'

The reporter was incredulous, saying he found it a rather odd directive, considering that Doris Day had been playing twenty-five-year-olds for two decades. Then he grinned. 'Hmm. The studio also lists your measurements as 34–22–35. Is that also a fabrication?'

We both burst out laughing, and I said emphatically, 'Of course *that's* accurate.'

My age wasn't the first thing the studio changed. One day shortly after I was hired to play Liesl, Bob Wise took me aside and said, 'Charmy, what would you think about changing your name?'

'My name?'

'Your last name.' He went on to explain. 'Charmian' was enough of a mouthful for him. With 'Farnon,' he felt, it was a tongue twister: Charmian Farnon. 'I think a one-syllable last name would be to your benefit.'

'That would be all right with me,' I said.

A few days later he handed me a long list of single-syllable last names, saying, 'Pick three.'

It had never occurred to me to change my name, but the idea had enormous appeal. Underneath it all, even though I'd never articulated it, I was angry with my father for disappearing from my life. Changing my last name would be a way to reinvent myself, to move past him. I went home and studied the list and finally chose three names. I don't remember the first two, but the third one was Carr, and out of the three I chose, that was Bob's favorite. That is how I became known as Charmian Carr. Shortly thereafter, my sister Darleen took the name Carr as well.

It took me a while to get used to my new last name. Often, I'd be sitting at the studio and hear a page for 'Miss Carr' several times before I would realize they were calling for me. But eventually it became a part of me, as when you take a new name in marriage – except, of course, this was a made-up name. Over the years, so many people with the last name Carr have written to me suggesting that we're related. And I have to laugh and respond that we're related 'in name only.'

It can be dangerous to overhaul your identity. It starts subtly, innocuously. You agree to change your name. Then, before you know it, other things about you are changed. Your age. Stories about how you were hired. What you like and dislike. Things about your personal life. Stories about whom you're dating. Whom you're in love with.

For a while, I looked at it as all part of a necessary game. If the studio felt the need to make me more intriguing, if they thought it would inspire more people to go see our film, then who was I to say that they had no right to make up stories about me? But it's like my image preserved on film: I learned that those fabrications will be with me forever.

If there was a downside to having been Liesl, it was the times when I felt smothered by the fiction, with my own identity buried beneath a pile of very public misinformation. I began to sense that when I was in public people expected me to *be* Liesl. I felt I had to dress up nicely and put on makeup, even to go to the grocery store, lest I disappoint someone and destroy the illusion. Sometimes the weight of expectations, the public scrutiny, seemed too much to bear. But I thought that if I stood up and shouted, 'These things you're reading about me are not true!' I would be letting everyone down – not just the studio, but fans. For a brief time, 'Liesl' began to feel like my evil twin, the perfect one, the one that everybody really loved. These feelings ultimately went away, but I'd be less than honest if I didn't say that, though I have always been proud to have been a part of *The Sound of Music*, there were times when I resented 'Liesl' as if she were a real person. She not only controlled my professional life but infiltrated my personal life as well, blurring the lines between who I was and who people expected me to be.

The Sound of Music *represents different things to different people. To many, like a writer I know, the story carried profound lessons.*

'*I was nine when my father died in 1965. The* Sound of Music *premiered on the day of his funeral. Several months later, when I saw the movie with my mother, the story had a strong impact upon me.*

'*My dad had never been particularly demonstrative. He was a typical father for that era, and left the chores of child-rearing to my mother. Fathers weren't encouraged to be involved in their children's lives, nor was it acceptable for them to display their feelings. But, like most kids, I wanted his attention, his praise, his affection. When he died, it seemed as if I would never be able to know how he truly felt about me.*

'*In a strange way, the film helped. Watching the moment when the father reached out to his children played out my own fantasy of connecting with my dad. And it did something more. There was a hidden message underlying that scene, that moment. Even though the Captain was distant and aloof, deep down he really did love his children. Their singing brought his true feelings to the surface.*

'*But what if the Captain had never heard his children's voices? What if he had remained distant? I realized that, even if the Captain had never expressed how he felt, his love for them was still there.*

180

'The Sound of Music *gave me this clue about fathers: just because they don't say something doesn't mean they don't feel it. I grew up believing that my father was the same kind of man as Captain von Trapp. We just never had a chance to sing together.*'

THE SOUND OF FATHERS

T wentieth Century Fox took advantage of every opportunity to keep me in the public eye to promote the film after it was released. They would send me to various high-profile events, and one evening in early 1966, they sent me to the premiere of a new film in Hollywood. There was a live orchestra playing at the party that followed, and I gave the conductor a second glance and realized – it was my father.

I hadn't seen him in nine years. At first I wasn't sure what to do, but I finally went over and said simply, 'Hello.'

He turned to me with some surprise and then said, 'Hi, Charmy! How've you been?' very nonchalantly, as if we were casual acquaintances. It was an eerie echo of *The Sound of Music*, in which a father is estranged from his children. Despite my lack of acting experience, I could play Liesl's relationship with her father without doing any research.

There were things that were never discussed when I was growing up, things I never asked about until decades later. If I had known more about my parents' history, perhaps I would have understood their problems, their choices. Instead, when Dad left and Mom would stare into a glass of smoke-colored booze, trying to make it from sunset till dawn, I would wonder why – or, worse, I would assume the cause was me.

My father, Brian Farnon, was born in Toronto but spent part of his childhood in Yorkshire, England, and Banbridge, Northern Ireland. I knew he was the oldest son in a large family, but I never once heard him talk about his childhood. He and his brothers were self-taught musicians, and his younger brother Robert eclipsed him early on, becoming the lead trumpet and top arranger for Percy Faith. My uncle later played with Dizzy Gillespie, in 1942 became the director of the Canadian Allied Expeditionary Forces Band (its American counterpart was directed by Glenn Miller), and after the war became a well-known composer and a conductor of the London Philharmonic Orchestra.

My father loves music. It defines who he is, inside as well as out. I believe it's the only thing he truly loves; it's more important to him than any wife or child. I don't say that out of bitterness, but in my effort to understand his choices. He didn't go to my daughter Emily's wedding simply because his band had a gig that day. To him, missing the chance to play music was unthinkable. Lately I find myself wondering if I should still hold these failings against him, or if I should accept him for who he is, gifted and flawed. He is at heart a wonderful person, generous and warm and funny. He's just not a great father or husband.

Shortly after I was born, my father left to tour

186

with his brother in the Canadian military band. When I finally met him again two years later, I didn't like him at first. He was a stranger, and I cried whenever he picked me up. But after a while he became my favorite person in the whole world. I had dimples just like his, so I felt I was his twin. I would mimic him, trying to do everything exactly the way he did. He had a unique way of clearing his throat, and I would practice clearing my own throat, trying to sound just like him. Not only did I mimic his gestures, but I also adopted his beliefs. He believed in extraterrestrials, so I did, too. He would tell me about reincarnation and say that, during this life, he was paying for his past lives.

'What do you mean?' I would ask. 'How have you paid?'

My father would only shrug.

I wouldn't learn what he meant until I was almost fifty years old. I was going through a horrible time, a time when things that I'd buried were surfacing, and one day I called my dad, wanting answers, needing answers.

He was angry at first, believing I was blaming him for the depression I was going through. I had to reassure him that I was only trying to sort out my own issues. Then he began to talk to me openly, for perhaps the first time in my life, and over the course of an hour I learned more about my father than I ever knew before.

When he was twelve, my dad was playing in the backyard of his parents' house in Toronto. He put a broomstick between two chairs and jumped over the stick, back and forth. His mother watched him from an upstairs window, laughing, and when his father came home from work, he watched him for a moment, then said, 'Let me try that, Brian.'

Dad's mother yelled down at her husband, 'Don't you dare do that! It's dangerous. It's too high for you!'

But Dad's father wanted to see if he could clear that hurdle. He leapt up, but his feet caught in the broomstick and he crashed to the cement. The fall ruptured his appendix. This was in 1923, before antibiotics, and there was nothing the doctors could do. They tried to drain some of the poison out, but three days later he died.

'He was the most wonderful man,' Dad said. 'I really loved him. It took me a long time to realize it wasn't my fault, that it was just an accident.'

After his father's death, there was no longer a man in the house, no one to provide financial support, and at the time there was no such thing as life insurance, or welfare, in Canada. His mother had to get a job, as did my dad at the age of thirteen.

'When Mum got a job, she put my other sister in a home,' Dad said.

I paused for a moment, confused. 'What other sister?' In my dad's family there had always been just my Aunt Nora, my father, my Uncle Bob, and my Uncle Dennis. Here I was, middle-aged and suddenly discovering I had another aunt, a ghost from the past.

'Her name was Eileen.'

'Why was she put in a home?'

'She was slow. Mum worried that, while she was at work all day, people might take advantage of Eileen. She needed to be someplace where she'd be safe. Mum found this really nice home, and Eileen stayed there.'

'But what happened to her?'

'She died there, I think.'

'You think?'

I listened to the silence that followed, and sensed that bound up in his father's death and his sister's loss was a pain Dad had buried so deep he never dealt with it.

'My mother was never happy after that,' he said. 'She never really smiled again.' His words were casual, as if it didn't matter, as if it had never mattered. But I began to understand. My father's ability to sever these painful memories, to cast them adrift like unwanted cargo, explained to me how he could leave us. This was the only way he knew how to cope, to survive.

In *The Sound of Music*, the father suddenly realizes how he has cut himself off from his children. He reaches out to them, joining them in song. Many people have been deeply moved by that scene, perhaps because they identify with the difficult relationship that can exist between parent and child. In real life, our fathers' songs can be less clear, the resolution less specific.

My father is a musician. Notes flow from him,

as if from God, and I try to listen now and understand. Unlike Captain von Trapp, my father never saw what losing him did to me. He never realized how, ignoring his own pain, tossing it aside, he merely inflicted it upon me, upon us. He never saw how much my sisters and I needed him and wanted to be close to him. The irony for me is that, whereas music brought the Captain and his children together in the story, in my real life music has at times kept my father and me apart.

But he is my father. I love him. I love his music. And, as with the von Trapp children, perhaps the best way I can connect with him is by speaking to him in the only language he understands. It is a language without words – only notes.

*O*n the surface, **The Sound of Music** *is just a movie, a simple story. But for many, the film provided insights about others in their lives, like the widow who shared this story.*

'My husband has been dead for four years. Like many couples, we had our ups and downs. He was a hard man to know at times. He was talkative, but not about his deepest feelings. After over forty years of marriage, I can't honestly say I really knew him.

'He was a John Wayne kind of man. He hunted and fished and loved movies like **High Noon**. But he was also a closet **Sound of Music** fan. Every year he'd watch it when it was on television. Heaven help anyone who made a peep in the family room when it was on. He'd glare at them, or even ask them to leave, he'd be so immersed in that story.

'His love of that film is a window for me to understanding the parts of him he could never talk about. It's a story about love, not only romantic love, but also the love of a father for his children.

'Our three children had difficulty in their relationships with him at times, particularly our daughter. I think that movie was so special to him because that was his fantasy – to be able to reach out somehow and bridge the gulf between them, to express his feelings and have them reciprocated.

'I suppose it's sad to need a film to gain some

191

insights into a man I knew for over four decades. But marriage and raising a family are not always easy things. Sometimes the only way we can understand our own experiences is through stories that come from outside our own walls.'

MARRIAGE AND FAMILY

Almost the entire time I was in Salzburg, when I wasn't working on the movie, I was working for Twentieth Century Fox on a documentary film called *Salzburg: Sight and Sound*. This twenty-minute short film was released into theaters months before *The Sound of Music* premiered.

One of the first mini-documentaries of its kind, it showed behind-the-scenes footage of *The Sound of Music* while it was being shot. It must have been the longest commercial ever made, and not just because it was a trailer. Sponsored in part by Pan Am airlines (which no doubt hoped to promote European tourism), the film shows me wandering amid the attractions of Salzburg with a blue-and-white Pan Am bag slung over my shoulder.

The only person I know who paid any attention to this little documentary was a man who watched it in a theater one night while waiting for the main feature to come on. He would later tell me that he sat up when I came on the screen and thought, 'What a pretty girl.' He was a dentist in Encino, and he rarely went out to movies.

One question I was always asked when I was touring with the film was, 'What's your ambition in life?'

I always answered it the same way: 'I want to do more acting, but ultimately I want to get married and have a family.'

Mickey Levey, Harry's son, the man who'd been my boyfriend for so long, knew before I did that *The Sound of Music* was going to change our relationship. While I was traveling for the film, Mickey wrote me that he had a surprise for me when I returned home. It turned out to be an engagement ring.

I didn't know what to say. I didn't feel I was ready to get married, but I loved Mickey. He was a wonderful, sweet young man. Having recently lost his father, he was, I knew, afraid of losing me, too. I said, 'Yes.' During the time we were engaged, we took a long trip together, which was incorporated into my traveling for Twentieth Century Fox. We went all through the Caribbean and to New York, and it was great fun. But by the time we returned home, I knew I wasn't ready to get married. I gave Mickey back his ring.

We remain good friends to this day, and I still get together with him and his wife occasionally. One day in the spring of 1966, we were having lunch in a restaurant, and there across the room was the doctor I had been working for when I was hired to play Liesl. He saw us, so we stopped by his table as we were leaving.

He introduced us to the young man he was dining with, a dentist named Jay Brent. And I said, 'You're a dentist? You know, I need to see a dentist before I leave on this trip. Is there any chance you could fit me in?'

He looked at me and recognized me – not from *The Sound of Music*, which I later learned he'd never seen, but from the documentary *Salzburg: Sight and Sound*. A moment passed before he stammered, 'Uh . . . there's no way I can fit you into my schedule . . .' I smiled at him, and he paused before finishing: '. . . unless you want to go to my office right now, during my lunch hour.' He got right up and we went to his office. That is how Jay and I met. We would be married for almost twenty-five years.

He claims he tried to be 'cool' that day and not rush things, so he waited two whole hours after he worked on my teeth before he called to ask me out.

At the time, I was still traveling a lot for the film, so I ended up breaking several dates with him. But when we managed to get together, I really enjoyed his company. When he asked me to marry him, I said, 'Yes.'

We picked October 31 as the big day and ordered our invitations. But then I was hired to do a television play called *Evening Primrose* for the dramatic anthology series 'ABC Stage 67.' The three-week shoot in New York City stretched to six, and I wouldn't be back in time for the wedding and honeymoon. So Jay and I postponed our plans indefinitely.

Evening Primrose was fabulous fun. It was an

avant-garde story written by James Goldman and Stephen Sondheim. Anthony Perkins plays a rundown poet who decides that he can hide in a department store, sleep during the day, and have peace and quiet to write poems every night. But he discovers the store is full of other people doing the same thing, posing as mannequins during the day and living their lives out when the store closes at night.

I played the part of a young girl held captive by this strange band of department-store squatters for more than ten years. Tony's character falls in love with my character, and mine with his. But the story ends on a macabre note, as our characters try to escape and are murdered by the other denizens of the store. Tony and I end up as mannequins, posed as bride and groom in a display window. It was my second acting job after *The Sound of Music* (my first had been a black-and-white TV pilot for Fox called 'Take Her, She's Mine' with Van Johnson, which was based on the James Stewart–Sandra Dee movie but failed because most sitcoms that year were shot in color).

Evening Primrose confirmed for me that I still wanted to pursue acting. And I adored Tony Perkins. He was absolutely gorgeous, but he wasn't the least bit interested in me. I flirted endlessly, smiled shyly, tried to be engaging in every conversation, all to no avail. Still, I would open up newspapers when I was in New York, and there would be a story about Tony and me having dinner together the night before, or going out on a date to the theater. We were supposed to be madly in love. Of course it was studio publicity – something I was all too familiar with.

I returned home to Los Angeles, and Jay and I decided to go ahead with our marriage. After our wedding in May of 1967, we spent two weeks in Tahiti, then visited Hawaii on the way back home. We traveled extensively during the first couple of years of our marriage, and everywhere we went, 'Liesl' followed. Once, in Jamaica, we were waterskiing and I was wearing a hat and sunglasses – I think I even had zinc oxide on my nose – when a boat began following us. When it caught up to us, the people on board asked, 'Are you Liesl? Can we get your autograph?'

Jay and I could only share an incredulous look.

I figured that since he was married to me Jay should at least see *The Sound of Music*, so I took him to a screening on the Fox lot. He thought it was good, but he didn't go crazy about it; it didn't change the way he looked at me. Shortly afterward, I became pregnant with our first child, and Jay and I agreed that I would give up acting in films.

And I have no regrets. Acting in a film takes you away from your family. Even under the best of circumstances, you are gone, not only physically, but also emotionally. When you are working on a film, you become totally immersed in it. It's the first thing you think about when you wake up in the morning, and you focus on it until the minute you go to bed. There's little time for much else, and children, by necessity, often take a back seat. I knew I couldn't be a good actress and a mother. Perhaps others could – but I couldn't.

I know this: my children would have had very different childhoods had I not stopped working in films. I'm positive of this. Instead, our two daughters became the center of my life. They have grown up into two amazing young women.

Though he didn't want me to work, Jay was supportive of me as a person, particularly when my mother was not. One night we had dinner at my mother's house, and a friend of Mom's who was there started to talk about *The Sound of Music.*

'Charmy,' she said, 'you were so great as Liesl. I still love to see that movie whenever it's out. And you've grown into such a wonderful woman, with your two beautiful daughters and everything else you've accomplished . . .' She went on for a minute or two, saying some very nice things.

Mom waited until she was finished and then said, 'Good? You think Charmian is good? I'll tell you what she is. She's lucky! Just lucky. I got her the part in that movie. Anything else she's ever done is only because she was in *The Sound of Music.* She hasn't got any talent. She's just lucky.'

I stared down at my plate, and the room got very quiet. Mom had had a bit too much to drink. It was one of those awkward moments that I had grown used to over the years. Jay bit his lip, but later, in the car, he was furious. 'Your mother's wrong,

Charmy. You know she's wrong.' His support and words always helped.

When we found out I was pregnant, we bought a house in Encino, the house I still live in today, and before our baby was born we got a puppy, a black Lab that I named Beau. It was the only boy's name that I really liked, and I told Jay if we had a boy I'd name him Beau, too. Fortunately, we had a little girl whom we named Jennifer, and she was followed three years later by her sister, Emily.

The first time Emily saw me in *The Sound of Music*, she was just two years old. She kept toddling up to the TV every time Christopher Plummer appeared on the screen, asking me, 'Is zat you?'

I knew my looks had changed over the years, but I never really thought there was a resemblance between Chris Plummer and me. About the fifth time Emily asked me if I was Chris, I decided it was bed-time for Emily.

I don't think my role in the film had a particularly strong impact on either of my daughters. Many of their friends' parents were also in show business. And, as Jay is quick to point out, he began filming them from the moment they were born, so they'd been watching themselves in home movies and videos their whole lives. Seeing Mom, albeit a younger version, on television in *The Sound of Music* just wasn't a big deal. By the time they were old enough to watch it and understand that it wasn't like one of Dad's home movies, the film was more than a decade old, which to them was ancient. Occasionally someone at their school would get excited and ask them for my autograph, but apart from such moments, 'Liesl' was not a part of their lives. And they were much more aware of my work in commercials than in the film.

When Jennifer was a year old, I returned to acting part-time. I began to do commercials for products ranging from NyQuil to Sanka to Tollhouse Cookies. The girls frequently accompanied me on interviews, and sometimes even on shoots. But the thing they remember most is not my acting in front of cameras, but my taking them out for ice cream afterward.

The Sound of Music was neither Jennifer's nor Emily's favorite movie – not that I expected it would be. Interestingly, they both have the same favorite: *Somewhere in Time*.

'Favorite movie and favorite sound track,' they both agree.

Best *Sound of Music* memory? 'Having Nicholas Hammond tuck us in for bed.'

Emily nods. 'Having Spiderman put me to bed was very cool.' (They would watch Nicky on the TV series religiously.)

'I definitely had a crush on him,' Jennifer says.

'Me, too, but as Spiderman, not as Friedrich,' Emily agrees.

'You're right. He looked great in those blue-and-red tights.'

Despite their infatuation with 'Spiderman' and

other such influences in their childhood, neither of them pursued a career in show business. Jennifer is a businesswoman in the Bay Area and the mother of her own little girl, Emma. (Yes, Liesl is a grandmother!) And Emily is an architect, and lives not far from her sister. I am so proud of them both. I am proud of the choices they have made. I enjoy them as people. They are hardworking young women who lead full and productive lives. And I think they are wiser than I was at their age. Perhaps each generation feels this as they watch those who follow.

In 1991, after twenty-four years, my marriage to Jay fell apart. I always felt very loved by him, and very safe. At times my fame was hard on our relationship. It wasn't easy for him to have people literally turn their backs on him to talk to 'Liesl.' That happened to Jay frequently.

We couldn't work out our differences, but to me what's important is that our ties remain. We share a quarter-century of memories. And most important of all, we share our daughters. We flew together to be with Jennifer on the day when Emma was born, and will always be there, side by side, for the important moments in our daughters' lives.

Someone once told me that children are like kites. You struggle just to get them in the air; they crash; you add a longer tail. Then they get caught in a tree; you climb up and bring them down, and untangle the string; you run to get them aloft again.

Finally, the kite is airborne, and it flies higher and higher, as you let out more string, until it's so high in the sky, it looks like a bird. And if the string snaps, and you've done your job right, the kite will continue to soar in the wind, all by itself.

Jennifer and Emily are flying free now, with families of their own. They are the best part of my life. I will always be known to the world for my role in *The Sound of Music*. But to me, nothing I have ever done or ever will do in my life will be more important than my role as their mother. When Liesl tells Maria that she likes calling her 'Mother,' Maria says, 'I like hearing it.' And I know exactly what she means.

'*T*he first movie I ever saw was **The Sound of Music**. *I was only five, but I remember it to this day. I was afraid of heights, and there weren't any seats left in the lower section of the theater, so we had to sit in the balcony. I was so scared my mom had to hold me on her lap. I sat with my head pressed against her chest, but bit by bit, I peeked at what was happening on the screen. Then came the scene when Gretl holds up her hand to show Fraulein Maria she is five. I sat up and thought, "She's the same age as me!" From that moment on, I was totally immersed in the story, completely forgetting my fears.*

'*My parents bought the sound-track album and I would play it over and over. The cover had the usual credits for the actors and the director and the producer, but one name seemed to stick in my head to the exclusion of all others: Ernest Lehman, the man who wrote the screenplay. I can't explain why just him, why only his name.*

'*Three years later, when I saw the theatrical rerelease of the film* West Side Story, *the name ERNEST LEHMAN flashed across the screen during the credits and I exclaimed to my mom, "There's my friend!" Robert Wise and Saul Chaplin had also worked on both pictures, but for whatever reason, I hadn't noticed their names. Only "my friend."*

205

'The Sound of Music *remained my all-time favorite film. One day, long after I had graduated from college, I was visiting my former roommate from UCLA. She was an aspiring screenwriter, and she told me about this man, Ernie, who, through the Writers' Guild Bulletin Board on the Internet, was helping her with her screenplay. I didn't make the connection at first, until she mentioned his last name. I said, "Ernest Lehman?!"*

'I told her the story of how that name had always stuck with me, and she E-mailed Ernie and told him my story. A year later, I happened to be at my friend's place again, and she was chatting on-line with Ernie and had to dash somewhere and invited me to take her place. Timidly, I got on the keyboard to say hello to him for the first time. We are both very shy people, yet we had an instantaneous bond as we wrote back and forth. It was incredible. We began to "meet" every night on-line, and within three weeks, it was obvious to both of us that we had fallen in love with each other, even though we had never met.

'We were an unlikely couple at first. He was a widower, quite a bit older than me. I was interested in history and psychology more than filmmaking. But a month later, at a dinner party, when we finally met face to face, I felt like I had come home.

'I can't explain the forces that brought us together. I can't explain why his name jumped out at me from that album cover when I was just learning to read. But Ernest Lehman and I were married last year. The Sound of Music *brought us together. Ernie wrote a*

script that touched my soul, and years later I was led to him, as if by magic.'

—Laurie Lehman

INTERIOR BY DESIGN

Many things helped make *The Sound of Music* extraordinary. One of them was the set design. Boris Leven, a Russian immigrant who graduated from USC, was the man responsible for the gorgeous sets in the film. With the exception of Mondsee Cathedral and the Reverend Mother's office (which was filmed in Salzburg but on a soundstage), all the interiors were filmed on soundstages in southern California. Boris was able to make his sets so realistic that many viewers believed scenes shot in Los Angeles were done on location in Austria.

Perhaps it was because of the artistry of Boris Leven that I became interested in interior design, the field I have worked in for more than twenty years. My most famous client was a huge fan of the movie, so much so that, when he read in an article in the *Los Angeles Times* that 'Liesl' was married to a dentist in Encino, he himself bought property in Encino. He thought that if 'Liesl' lived there it must be a nice place to live.

In 1981, I was recommended to him as a designer, and he telephoned me. 'I can't believe you're going to decorate my house,' he said. '*The Sound of Music* is my favorite film. Whenever I'm depressed, I watch it. I've always loved Liesl.'

I was surprised by this revelation. It never occurred

to me that a rock star would love such a family-oriented film. When he said he wanted to sing me one of his favorite songs, I wasn't expecting to hear 'So Long, Farewell.' But that is what he began to sing to me, and soon we were singing songs from the film to each other over the phone. That is how my friendship with Michael Jackson began.

The eleven-thousand-square-foot house he was building was only half a mile away from my own home. He loved Disneyland and wanted to capture some of the unique magic of the park at his estate. Together, over several years, we transformed his home into an enchanting palace with a cascading waterfall and a candy store and outdoor lighting that made the grounds magical after dark.

Much of the design was whimsical and fun. It was Michael's idea to decorate his bedroom with mannequins: 'I want it to look like there's a party going on.' So we found seven adults and ten children in different poses. His mom and his sister LaToya and I went shopping for their clothes and back at the house spent hours dressing the mannequins. When the room was done, it *did* look as if a party was going on. One guy was sitting on the hearth and I accidentally bumped into him and said, 'Sorry,' before I remembered he wasn't real.

There was a large room off the kitchen that Michael wanted to look like the ride 'The Pirates of the Caribbean' at Disneyland. 'Which part of the ride do you want it to look like?' I asked. 'The beginning scene in the bayou? The mounds of treasure? The ship firing at the fort? The town being looted?' Michael couldn't decide. So we went to Disneyland, not just once, but several times over the next two years.

The first couple of times we visited the theme park, it was before the release of *Thriller*, and we were able to walk around the park with just a handful of fans stopping him. But after *Thriller*, it became almost impossible for us to walk more than ten feet without his being accosted.

Still, Michael refused to go to the park as a VIP. 'It wouldn't be the same,' he'd explain. 'If I can't go around like everyone else, if they take me to the front of the line and lead me through the private passages, well, to me that's not fair to everyone who's waiting. And it's no longer Disneyland to me.' So we always went right up to the front gate, bought our tickets, and tried to walk down the middle of Main Street like everyone else. Michael took to wearing jokey disguises like those plastic glasses with the bushy eyebrows and the nose and mustache – the Groucho Marx look. I don't think anybody was fooled, but the whole point was to have some fun. Michael loved to have a good time. He didn't want to be catered to; he wanted to be treated like everyone else. I always loved those trips to Disneyland with him, watching how much he enjoyed going on the rides. I must admit, however, that 'The Pirates of the Caribbean' wore a little thin after a while. 'Yo ho! Yo ho! The pirate's life for me . . .' I would hear the music in my dreams. After all those times on the ride, Michael still couldn't decide which part he wanted to have duplicated in the big room off his kitchen.

While working for Michael, I had an opportunity to meet some special people. One in particular I'll never forget: Jacqueline Kennedy Onassis. Michael was going to do a book about his life, and she was his editor at Doubleday. She flew out from New York to meet with him at his house, and he asked me to be there. Michael was very shy when he first met people, so he liked having a friend around.

It had been crazy at his house, getting ready for her visit. Michael's eight-foot-long python had escaped from its glass cage. We were in a panic trying to locate it before Jackie arrived. We kept finding snakeskin all over the place (it was molting), but no snake. Then, when all seemed lost, we found the snake in Michael's arcade room, curled up in the cockatoo cage. The bird was nowhere in sight, and the snake had a suspicious lump in its middle. Found the snake, lost the cockatoo.

Jackie arrived right on time. She was so elegant, dressed in a black cashmere turtleneck and pants, and I couldn't take my eyes off her as she shook hands with Michael. He then turned to me and said, 'This is Charmy.'

She reached out her hand, and said, 'Hello, I'm Jacqueline Onassis.'

All I could do was whisper, 'I know.'

I loved working on Michael's house. It challenged me and stretched my imagination, and I view the finished product as some of my best work. Other clients have included members of my *Sound of Music* family. I worked with Angela Cartwright and her husband, Steve, during a reconstruction of their house. And I helped Ernie Lehman remodel his bungalow. I'll never forget when he called me.

'Charmy?'

'Hi, Ernie!'

'I have some news. I'm going to get married . . .'

His wife, Jackie, had died after a long bout with Alzheimer's and cancer. Ernie had taken such good care of Jackie when she was sick, absolutely doting on her. Now, approaching eighty, he was embarking on a new marriage. He paused for a moment on the phone, before saying, 'I'm thinking I ought to redo the bedroom . . .'

I was more than happy to work with him. Not that working with Ernie is easy – ask any Hollywood producer. The first time he met Bob Wise is a good example. Ernie himself remembers the moment well.

'My phone rang in my office at MGM. I was polishing the final script of *Executive Suite*, when the producer of the film, John Houseman, called to say, "I've got our director, Bob Wise, here in my office. Come on up and meet him." So I went up, and there was Bob Wise. We shook hands, and I sat down, and John Houseman was proudly leafing through the screenplay, and he mentioned this one scene. And I said, "Forget about that scene, John, I'm going to rewrite it." Houseman grew purple. He stood up and leaned over his desk and shouted at me, "Lehman! You are a barbarian going at the Hope Diamond with an ax!" Those were his exact words. Then he banished me from the room, shouting, "Go back to your office!" I slunk back to my desk, and couldn't imagine what Bob Wise must have thought. But everyone was always sending me back to my office.'

I hold Ernie Lehman's volume of work in such high regard, and feel that all of us involved in *The Sound of Music* owe him a true debt. Still, there were times during my remodeling of his house when *I* thought about sending him back to his office.

We were going to reupholster the couch in his bedroom, so I brought him fabric samples. I found a pattern I thought would complement his other choices. 'Too dull!' he pronounced. 'I like color. I like things to be bold!' He picked a fabric that shouted from the sample book. After the upholstering was done, and the couch had sat in his room for a couple of days, he called. 'Charmy, this couch is awful.'

'Well, gee, Ernie, I . . .'

'How about that fabric you showed me? Why didn't we go with that?'

'Uh . . .'

The couch was redone in the material I'd suggested. After his bedroom was finished, he decided to redecorate his kitchen. I held a sample paint chip against the wall. 'Ernie, how about this soft yellow?'

'No. I want it bright. Bright yellow.'

'I think you'll find that'll be too loud.'

'I like things bright!' We went around and around about the color of the paint. He finally had the room done in a bold yellow.

He called me not long after the kitchen was done. 'Charmy, we've got to do something about this kitchen. I feel like I'm living inside a giant lemon!'

'Ernie, I . . .'

'How about something softer?'

The kitchen was repainted in the muted color I'd originally suggested. Ernie smiled when it was done. 'This is much better. I told you the other color was going to be too bright.'

'Ernie . . .'

'Charmy, did I ever tell you about the other decorator I had before you? She fired me. One day she just yelled, "Ernie, you're fired!" Can you believe that?'

'Well . . .'

'I mean, *I* hired *her*!'

Ernie Lehman always keeps me on my toes – and working for him is anything but dull.

My best clients ever were, and are, Bob and Heather (née Menzies; she played Louisa) Urich. I've worked with them on several homes. When Bob was doing the television series 'Spenser: For

Hire,' the show was filmed entirely on location in Boston. Heather and Bob fell in love with a 150-year-old house in Andover, situated on twenty acres of rolling hills, a perfect place for Heather to hunt and jump her horse, Baron von Trapp. The house was a three-story stick-and-shingle neo-classic and, because of its age, necessitated a complete overhaul, from the inside out. Before redecorating, pipes and wires and interior walls needed replacing.

One small annoyance caused continual frustration. Bob and Heather wanted to put in a window over the sink of a small downstairs powder room. For some reason the architect didn't put it in his plans, and the contractor, despite Bob's gentle reminders, went ahead and drywalled the room – without a window. Finally, Bob, who is a man of action, picked up a big sledgehammer, calmly went into the powder room, told the contractor, 'I want a window right here,' and swung the sledge-hammer against the spot above the sink. A huge hole appeared in the drywall exactly where they wanted the window – and the window was installed!

The best thing that came out of my being a decorator is a love story. A dear old friend, Libbie, was having the most horrible year of her life. Her daughter had become ill, and then her best friend had died of a heart attack in Santa Fe. Libbie flew from L.A. to New Mexico only to have her flight diverted by a bad snowstorm. She was rerouted back to Los Angeles. It was pouring rain as she drove home, depressed, and she decided to make a fire in the fireplace and curl up in bed. She stopped by a market and picked up one of those self-burning logs.

Snuggling under the covers, she was staring at the fire when the log exploded into a thousand pieces with such force that the embers blew through the fire screen. The carpet in her bedroom caught fire. She jumped out of bed, with one hand dialing 911 and with the other trying to keep the fire at bay with a fire extinguisher.

Though firemen saved the rest of the house, the interior of her bedroom was destroyed. So, just weeks before Christmas, I got a call from Libbie. 'Can you handle this right now?' I quickly redesigned the room, helped her pick out some new furnishings, and got subcontractors to start repairing the damage immediately. I hired Guy, a painter I had used several times before, and who I knew would get the job done perfectly and quickly.

When I introduced them, I had no idea that Libbie looked into his blue eyes – and fell in love. She'd never had such instant feelings for anyone before, and at first she tried to ignore them. But every day, when she came home from work, Guy was there finishing up, and she was so glad to see him. Then, on New Year's Eve, she came home and he was gone, his work completed. She realized she would never see him again – and she also realized that she couldn't live with that thought. She called me and casually said, 'Charmy, what can you tell me about Guy?'

'Didn't he do a good job?'

'Oh, yes, he did great.' She hesitated. 'Charmy, I think I'm in love with him.'

A week later, she called him and invited him out for dinner, and it turned out that everything she was feeling for him, he was feeling for her. They haven't been apart since.

Some friends gave her a hard time. 'Libbie? A housepainter?'

Perhaps Georg von Trapp received the same type of comments. 'Georg? A governess?'

Libbie and Guy remind me a bit of the main characters in the film. They were brought together when one was hired to work at the other's home. A miracle happened: they fell in love, and their lives were altered forever, in the most positive way.

Libbie has told me that if she hadn't been in such a vulnerable state she might have denied the feelings welling up inside her. Perhaps it is only when we most need them that our own interiors become visible to us, and we can see the path that God has designed for us all.

*S*ometimes *I made very special friends because of the movie, as the following story illustrates.*

'I was seventeen when I first saw The Sound of Music *in 1965. The film touched me to the core. I went to see it twice, which was unusual for me. Everything about it appealed to me. It was about a close family that was bound by honor and, facing overwhelming forces, managed to prevail.*

'And I loved Liesl. She was beautiful, of course, but there was something else about her, a sense of courage, yet a vulnerability that was attractive. She was my heroine. It was my teenage fantasy to be the one who would protect her, to stand between her and the Nazis and make sure nothing ever happened to her.

'More recently, I saw a film called The Postman *with Kevin Costner. It's a postapocalyptic tale, a grim view of the world in the future. There was one scene that struck me. An evil warlord is showing films to his conscription army at his rock quarry encampment. The projectionist puts on a violent war movie and the horde boos and hisses. But then he puts on* The Sound of Music, *and this war-torn group of soldiers sits back, mesmerized. That is the fantasy they want, a return to the kind of world the film depicts, a world of beauty and honor, where family and love and principles prevail. The moment works in the film because* The Sound of Music *really does have that kind of enduring appeal.*

221

'Reality can sometimes match fantasy. I'm a surgeon, and one day I was about to meet with a referred patient. Before I went into the examination room, I glanced at her chart and read the name "Charmian Carr." And I thought, It can't be. But when I opened the door, I saw that indeed it was. It was Liesl.

'It isn't often that we get to meet the objects of our youthful fantasies, and I suppose it's even rarer that they end up being the kinds of people we imagined them to be. Charmian, like the character she had portrayed, was charming and lovely and also courageous. I didn't get to save her from any bad guys. But it was nice to be able to fix her knee.'

MY FAVORITE THINGS

When the von Trapp children are frightened by a thunderstorm, Maria encourages them to think of things that make them happy. 'I simply remember my favorite things, and then I don't feel so bad.' It's marvelous advice, yet, in the middle of my own life's 'storms,' such words seemed trivial.

I went through a difficult period during my late forties. My impending divorce from Jay, as well as issues from my past, became overwhelming, making me feel anxious and profoundly depressed. For a long time I tried to ignore my feelings and bury myself in my work. But ultimately, to paraphrase the Reverend Mother, I couldn't shut out my problems. I had to face them.

Much of my midlife sadness was tied to events of long ago, and to resolve what was happening to me meant confronting my past. Perhaps, to understand ourselves truly, we must reach back to our parents and grandparents, to discover the forces that shaped them, and that end up shaping us. I began to ask questions I'd never asked before, of both my parents and myself.

I have no memory of crying when my father left our family. I wanted everything to go on as it always had, with everyone happy. If I had any strength growing up, it was in my ability to 'not see,' to pretend that all was well, that nothing hurt. In a newspaper interview for *The Sound of Music* in 1965, I told a reporter, 'I haven't seen my father in years . . . but I have no trauma about it.' This was what I said to everyone – including myself. Yet burying feelings about my father's leaving and my mother's subsequent bitterness didn't mean I'd ever resolved those issues. Out of the blue, it seemed, my past came back to haunt me.

I was suddenly afraid of things that had never bothered me before. The very thought of being in an elevator could provoke panic. Air travel became nearly impossible. I'd been the film ambassador who loved to fly – the more turbulence, the better. Overnight, I changed so that just stepping into a plane put me into a cold sweat. In the middle of it all, I injured my knee in a skiing accident and was told I should never dance again. Dancing had always been my escape, a large part of my identity. I didn't know how I'd survive without it.

Added to all my fears was a sinking sense of depression. I hated that this was happening to me. I couldn't understand it. I had so much to be thankful for. As everyone said, I had lived a charmed life. But mixed into the wonderful times of my life have been painful losses, not only my father leaving and my own divorce, but also the loss of members of our family.

Both of my sisters had sons. Sharon had Jeremy, along with his twin sister, Julie, and Darleen had

Zevan, her only child. They were all beautiful children, with marvelous personalities and gifts.

Zevan died when he was only two years old. The last half of his short life was fraught with illness, and it has never been positively determined what caused the immune deficiency that took his life. An incredibly bright little boy, he astounded me with the range of his vocabulary, and always melted me with his smile and his wise green eyes. Darleen called him her spirit child. I was with her at the hospital when Zevan died, and felt so helpless as I watched her rock him in her arms.

After he died, I couldn't stop crying. I believed if I could survive watching my sister lose her only child I would grow strong and never be so vulnerable again. But then, many years later, we lost Jeremy, too.

He was a grown man of twenty-four, so handsome and kind to everyone, when he was killed in a skiing accident. His life held such promise, and his death was so shattering, so fast, so unexpected. My sister Sharon's life changed in an instant, and I felt rocked to the core by the loss of this very special young man, and by my sister's deep pain.

His twin sister, Julie, was inconsolable. She crawled into his bed and refused all food and drink. We rallied around her. Darleen told her, 'Julie, now is the time to put your faith into practice.'

On the third day, I went into Jeremy's room to talk to my niece. And in that moment, I realized I *had* gained strength from our earlier loss of Zevan. I told Julie to look at me. I was dressed. I wasn't hiding under the covers. There were people who were at the house who needed to see her, to see us all. 'Look at the hurt they have,' I told her. 'You can help them.' I knew Julie wanted to die herself. I knew she was in deep pain. But I had learned that when tragedy strikes there is no alternative but to find the will to go on.

When I played Liesl, life was simple. The movie has a happy ending. But in real life, tragedy finds us. It found the real von Trapps. Their story continued. Captain von Trapp died only three years after the end of World War II. Martina, his youngest daughter by his first wife (little Gretl in the film), died just three years later, while giving birth to her first child. Yet the von Trapps survived. Inevitably all families face such struggles.

There's nothing worse in life than a parent's losing a child. My sisters will never get over the deaths of their sons. But they have taught me, through their strength and wisdom, how to take the most horrible of circumstances and try to make something positive out of it. And their sons, too, became my teachers. Zevan taught me that life is precious and to cherish every day. Jeremy made me realize that you never know what's going to happen, what's around the bend. The little irritations that crop up every day are meaningless. When such frustrations arise now, I do a reality check. I think of Zevan and Jeremy, and the anger or frustration I feel disappears. They have taught me to appreciate life.

And I've learned not to give up or give in to life's travails. With the assistance of my dear friend, director Robert Wise, I found a remarkable surgeon who operated on my knee, and later inspired me to do everything within my power to dance again. After more than a decade without dancing, I was finally able to return to it, with passion.

As I worked through my issues, I had a revelation. 'Maria's' advice about remembering and focusing on one's favorite things is not so trivial after all. I found that, on days when I was down, my favorite things could lift me up. I love children and Labradors, dark chocolate and gardening in the sun, a good steak with a bottle of wine and a house full of friends reminiscing about good times.

At the core of all that brightens me is music. It is such a magical force. If I'm blue, I can put on some music and dance or just listen, and I'm always inspired. I realized what a powerful antidote music has always been for me.

I realized something else, too. *The Sound of Music* has been – and continues to be – a strong thread running throughout my entire adult life. There have been times when I was frustrated that a character I played when I was twenty-one would define me for the rest of my days. I have long known that nothing I ever do professionally will eclipse my role as Liesl. But I began to realize that, rather than being a burden, this 'identity' was a gift. It gave me a special family that has always supported me through my good times – and bad.

On my coffee table is a glass obelisk that is etched with the words *The Earth has music for those who listen*. I learned, midlife, to listen to the music – and to appreciate those things that keep me going whenever there are thunderclouds on the horizon.

*I*t astounds me the number of people who feel the film changed the course of their lives. This music teacher from Minnesota is no exception.

'For thirty-four years, I've had a love affair with The Sound of Music. *Part of it's the mountains. When Maria says "That's my mountain" to the Reverend Mother, it makes me think of the hills of Oregon, where I grew up, and Mount Hood was my mountain.*

'*There is something about mountain peaks that's Godlike – I love the idea of freedom that they represent, the notion of being on top of the world and running free and singing with all my heart. At the very beginning of the film, as one vista of the Alps after another soars across the screen, those moments always affect me deeply. They are some of the most beautiful views of the earth.*

'*But it is the music that I treasure most about the film. Seeing* The Sound of Music *changed my life. It gave me a direction. Maybe I just wanted to be like Maria. After I saw the film, it became my life's work to teach children music.*

'*The Rodgers and Hammerstein score is so powerful. For more than thirty years I've used it in my teaching. There is no music I've found that affects children more than those* Sound of Music *songs. Children seem drawn to them, and singing them opens my students up, frees them.*

231

'We all need to touch the core of who we are – and to feel that beauty is attached to it. Everyone needs this, but especially children. When they sing those songs, they sense the beauty in themselves. That's the miracle of The Sound of Music. *It gives children a mountain to stand upon where they can see the beauty not only in the world but also in themselves.'*

CELLULOID SIBLINGS

When Central Casting put the seven of us children together as a fictional family, I don't think any of us had an inkling that a real family was being born. Yet that is what has happened in the years since we made *The Sound of Music*. I feel a very special bond with my six celluloid siblings. Since the day we first stood on a soundstage together, they have been my second family.

It doesn't always happen during the making of a film. The actors and crew generally work shoulder to shoulder for the duration of the job, then move on. The closeness we seven feel is rare.

Perhaps it happened because *The Sound of Music* was such a long shoot. We were together, almost nonstop, for months. Or maybe it was because the film was so successful that we have been frequently reunited through anniversary celebrations, and so became friends. Whatever the reason, I have a second family that I cherish.

Angela says she feels it's as if we're all part of a special club. Membership is experiential: you had to be there to be admitted in. She says no one else really understands what she's gone through except us – and her other second family from her years playing Penny Robinson on 'Lost in Space.' (Kym briefly joined Angela's 'Lost in Space' family when she guest-starred in an episode, as a princess who gets kissed by young Will Robinson, played by Billy Mumy. And Marta Kristen, before playing Judy on the show, had screen-tested for the role of Liesl. It's a small world, even if you're lost in space.)

But Angela's right. There are only six other people on the planet who know what it's like to have played one of Captain von Trapp's children in that film. No one else knows the inside jokes, the memories. Angela can say 'They're gone!' at the dinner table and instantly we all laugh, because we know she's imitating Alan Callow. We also know that if we let her she'll recite the whole script.

Someone will shout, 'Uh-oh. Stop her!'

'Quick! Change the subject!'

Angela grins, and does her best Fraulein Maria imitation. 'I could never answer to a whistle! Whistles are for dogs and cats and other animals, but not for children and definitely not for . . .'

'Angela!'

My closeness with my film family evolved as much after the filming was over as it did during. When we were in Salzburg, I traversed two worlds – in one I played a child, in the other I was an adult. At twenty-one, I was caught in between age groups, so I was frequently with the kids on the set, but off camera I was pulled in other directions. Too often I missed out on the fun the kids were having.

By union regulation, the children had to be in

school a minimum of three hours a day. The whole gang was frequently off on field trips while I was working on the documentary *Salzburg: Sight and Sound*. I envied them these excursions. They went to the salt mines, and later told me excitedly about the lakes they'd crossed inside a mountain, and the long wooden slides they'd used to get from one level to another. They went to the puppet show *The Magic Flute* and Mozart's birthplace and Hellbrun Castle. Kym still remembers their journey to 'Mad Ludwig's' citadel.

'I was only five, so I don't really remember everything about those days in Salzburg. But I clearly remember the castle, and what we learned about the king. He was crazy, and had devised all these gadgets and traps. I have strong visual memories of being there.' But, Kym says, 'most of my memories of that time are sensory. I remember the smell of the makeup and the gel they'd use on my hair. And, of course, the scent of fried artichokes.' She grins. 'And the costumes. They were made of the most beautiful fabrics. My favorite was the nightgown I wore in the thunderstorm scene. I loved it. I made drawings of all the costumes. I still have all these pictures I made in Salzburg.'

Though the kids were, for the most part, well behaved on the set, they were notorious for pulling pranks at their hotel in Salzburg. In the evening, as is Austrian custom, hotel guests would put their shoes outside their doors to be picked up and polished overnight. The kids, led by Nicholas Hammond, would race around switching the shoes, so in the morning none of the guests had the right pair.

I loved it years later when I read in Maria von Trapp's book about her first night in America. The whole von Trapp family was staying in a New York hotel, and they all placed their shoes outside their hotel-room door before they went to bed. The next morning, when they woke up and went to get their shoes, they were perplexed that no one had polished them. I wonder what Maria would have thought about the mischief the fictitious von Trapp children played upon the guests at the Hotel Mirabell.

The kids continued their pranks, bombing pedestrians below their windows with wads of soaked paper and generally wreaking havoc, until finally Bob Wise sat them down and reminded them that they were there to work, and if they didn't settle down, well . . .

That was all he had to say. We all lived in fear that we were replaceable – which I guess we were, though I have to imagine that by the time we were in Salzburg it would have been quite expensive to replace any of us.

The kids were a tight-knit group. They even created their own language so the adults wouldn't know what they were saying. They used it blatantly in front of us, giggling when we couldn't understand. Heather remembers the rules for it to this day. 'You put an "o" before every syllable and a "g" before every vowel. So Kym would be "okagim." Charmy would be "O-sh-gar-o-mie."'

They called it 'gibberish.' It was.

I remember how much the kids loved working with Julie Andrews. She would sing them songs and entertain them with stories and her two-ball juggling (demonstrated in the fruit-market scene), and the kids all fell in love with her, which I think shows in the film. Kym was totally enchanted by her: 'I just loved Julie.'

She taught them how to say 'supercalifragilistic-expialidocious' backwards, as only Mary Poppins could. Angela smiles, remembering. 'She tutored us on it for days. Not all of us could do it.'

Angela and Heather were nearly the same age, and became very close during the filming, a friendship that has continued in the years since.

'I was fourteen playing thirteen,' Heather points out.

'And I was twelve playing ten,' says Angela, nodding.

'It's funny how much the age difference mattered then. I mean, Kym was so little.'

'Now I'm a contemporary,' Kym reminds them, 'Though, of course, I'm still *much* younger.'

'We had a lot in common, Angela and I,' Heather remembers. 'We both had the biggest crush on the Beatles. I'll never forget the night we had an opportunity to go to see the Beatles at the Hollywood Bowl. We had an early-morning shoot the next day to film the scene where Maria sits on the pinecone. And we weren't allowed to go. I nearly rioted.'

The Beatles weren't the only idols they had a crush on. The two of them also had their eye on Dan Truhitte (Rolf). 'We never told him, but we did,' says Heather. 'We got over Dan, but I still love Paul McCartney.'

Heather and I are actually related. Not long ago, Heather was doing some genealogical research on her family and discovered we're distant cousins.

'See,' Heather says, smiling, 'we were meant to be family.'

Though the public-relations work surrounding the anniversaries of the film certainly helped bring us back together on many occasions, our families had already become close. We all lived in the Los Angeles area for a time, and our mothers would arrange barbecues and birthdays. I think we all went to every single birthday party Kym Karath had until she went off to college. That was one time when I knew I'd see everybody each year. Isn't that what families do? Getting together for birthdays and special occasions was how our relationship continued to evolve.

Being in the film had an impact on all of the kids. At times, Duane Chase felt having been Kurt was a bit of a burden. He didn't seek out recognition, and used to dislike it when strangers approached him. Being an actor was not what he wanted to do with the rest of his life. There were frequently long waits between scenes, especially during our gray days in Salzburg, and Duane often found his work on the film boring. One day, he just took off alone on a bicycle to tour around Salzburg, and everyone was in a tizzy trying to find him.

He did enjoy the technical aspects of movie-making, however. Betty Levin, the script supervisor, fondly remembers him following her around. 'Duane was very interested in what went on behind the camera. I'd turn around, and there he'd be. We'd talk about how all of this was going to be put together. It's no surprise to me that he's chosen to work in computers. You could see it in him on the set. He was bored with the enterprise of acting but loved learning how things worked. I remember when they let him operate the mike boom during one take. Now, *that* he was interested in.'

Kym was just starting elementary school when the film came out. 'That was hell,' she remembers. 'Other kids would tease me: "Oh, look, it's little Gretl!" They'd start singing my lines from "So Long, Farewell." It went on for years.'

Angela also remembers it wasn't easy. 'People think it must be great being in movies or on television. But it can be very tough on a child. I had two friends in school. That was it. There was a clique of girls that were brutal to me. They pulled some very mean stuff. My two friends got me through it. Without them, I would have been all alone.'

Heather had a different experience. 'I'd always been a wallflower. Shy. I didn't tell anybody I was doing this movie. I went away and they all thought I got pregnant or something. When I came back, I didn't tell anyone where I'd been. All of a sudden, the movie came out and all these people who never knew me, or cared to know me, were suddenly approaching me saying. "Oh, Heather, I've always thought you were so wonderful and you're my best friend." It was so transparent. Thank God for Angela. I didn't hang out with anybody from my school. Just Angela. I'd bike over to her house and we'd have slumber parties and play the guitar and sing. We were going to become rock stars so we could meet the Beatles.'

Maybe part of our bond was our individual frustrations with being 'trapped' by our roles. 'No one else can understand how difficult it can be – unless you've been through it,' Heather says. 'It sounds so trivial and trite, but the reality is, it affects you. As a young person you have to find your way through it. And it helped having our little family, the seven of us, to compare notes with.'

She continues. 'It was the worst for me when I entered adulthood. Even though I was doing Broadway shows and other roles, it was a constant battle to get past: "Oh – you're Louisa!" People would look me up and down and frown. "You don't look like her anymore." I'd see their disappointment and feel frustrated. I was letting people down because I wasn't thirteen years old anymore. It was as if they wished I'd been freeze-dried as Captain von Trapp's daughter. I rebelled for a while: I went out of my way to be totally different.'

Which does not mean that Heather walks around with this on her sleeve. She doesn't. None of my 'siblings' do. It was just something we each had to work through privately. It's the downside of being in such a successful film. But none of us would trade the overall experience for anything. We know how lucky we were to have been the von Trapp children. As with everything, there was a certain price attached, particularly when we were younger.

I've always been proud that we all survived the experience of success. Too often, child actors succumb to the pressures of early fame. All seven of us have done well and led good lives. No one's ever been in trouble. Everyone is a good citizen. We've talked about it over the years. None of us ever wanted to let the fans of the film down, to have someone open a newspaper to find that one of the 'von Trapp children' had been involved in something untoward. Nicky has said that being 'trapped' was a huge gift. 'I wanted to live up to the image. It made me try harder in all aspects of my life – not just professionally, but personally.'

Debbie Turner has lived in Minnesota for many years now, but she always makes a special effort to attend anniversary events. I don't think she's ever missed one. She grew up in a show-business family. Before Debbie ever played Marta, her older sister Patricia was cast as Linda Dennison, Beaver Cleaver's love interest on 'Leave It to Beaver.'

I recently had dinner with Debbie and Duane at a restaurant in New York. It was fun being with the two of them, at a table overlooking the Hudson River. It had been too long since we'd been together. Our talk ranged from politics and current events to our families. And I sat there thinking: who would have thought back in 1964 that we'd all still be together after all these years? Who would have thought that our fictional family would grow into a real one?

As the evening wore on, our discussion drifted, as it always does, to the memories we share of those long-ago days. Debbie leaned back in her chair and asked Duane, 'Do you remember when you built me that skateboard?'

'I do,' he admits. 'Can you ride it yet?'

'No.'

He shakes his head, grinning. 'Figures.'

'You were always building something. Or hanging out with the crew. You used to hang around Ted McCord so much.' (Ted was the cinematographer.)

Duane nods. 'I drove him crazy. But to this day, I remember the things he taught me. He used to tell me, "Duane, if you can see the camera, the camera can see you."'

'You know, I always thought you'd be a cameraman.'

'I was, Debbie. Don't you remember? When I

was sixteen, at your sister's wedding, your dad just handed me his Brownie movie camera and said, "Here, Duane, make a movie of this."'

'Gosh, I forgot all about that.'

'I've been meaning to ask. How'd that film turn out?'

Debbie shakes her head, grinning at him. It goes on and on like this.

The following night, all seven of us had an opportunity to be together. I always love such occasions, which have become rarer as we've scattered and become preoccupied with families and careers.

We all seem busier than ever these days. Nicky has lived in Australia for more than a decade, and is well known in theater and film Down Under. Since *The Sound of Music*, he has acted in twenty-eight movies and more than 150 television shows; now he does triple duty, not only acting, but also writing and producing.

Heather also did a great deal of acting after *Music*, with credits in everything from sitcoms to Broadway. Once she became a mom, though, she greatly curtailed her professional career. She and her husband, Robert Urich, have three children.

Duane worked as a petroleum geologist for many years, and now lives outside Seattle, where he works for a software company. He's married to a lovely woman, a nurse named Petra who used to be an Austrian nanny. He didn't intentionally seek out a 'Fraulein Maria' as his wife, but I've always thought it a sweet irony. And, as Duane notes, if you really want irony, Petra's middle name is Maria.

Angela was an old pro long before she was cast as Brigitta. She has dozens of film and television credits to her name, but once her son and daughter were born, she wanted a career that would allow her to be home to raise them. The store she opened two decades ago, Rubber Boots, has grown and is now also thriving on the Internet. In addition, Angela, who was always interested in photography, runs a portrait studio and does still-life photography.

Like Angela, Debbie is very artistic. The mother of four children, she has for years run her own business, an upscale floral-design company, and also works as a mortgage broker.

Kym continued to act after *The Sound of Music*. She made guest appearances on numerous episodic television shows, from 'My Three Sons' to 'Family Affair' to 'The Brady Bunch' (Nicky appeared with the Bradys as well). She went to USC, and after graduation continued to pursue acting jobs. Then, tiring of the Hollywood scene, she opted to move to Paris for a while, to study at the Art History School of the Louvre. When she returned to the States, she worked on 'All My Children.' Once her son was born, she took another break from acting.

I love that we have all chosen to stay in touch. Part of our bond defies words. It is just there, the result of many magic moments on the sets and the streets of Salzburg, of being part of a timeless film that continues to affect people to this day, and of watching each other grow and change over the years.

In many ways, I see no difference between my celluloid siblings and my real ones. We're all very different; some of us have closer relationships than others; but all seven of us have this bond. It is experiential, powerful, and ours alone. We know each other's histories, each other's strengths and weaknesses. We console each other during times of struggle and celebrate our moments of triumph – just like any other family.

A gentleman from Puerto Rico wrote to me in *1966, expressing his gratitude for the enchant-ing hours he'd spent watching the movie. He had seen the film eight times and felt it touched a special chord for his generation.* The Sound of Music *reflected for him many of the values that he had fought to preserve: love of country, love of freedom, and the preciousness of human dignity.*

He wrote that he had served overseas during World War II, and one day met a 'Rolf.' At the time, he was responsible for a unit of prisoners of war, and the boy was one of his charges. He was very young, probably no more than fourteen or fifteen, and was assigned to a work detail doing very heavy labor. The soldier felt sorry for him and decided to try to get the boy re-assigned.

He got an interpreter, brought the boy in to talk to him, and learned he was an Austrian. But when he asked the boy what he had done before the war, questioning him about his family and where he had gone to school, the boy spat out, 'School? I am a member of the Hitler Youth!' He added defiantly that he was a professional soldier. An Aryan. Glaring at the soldier from Puerto Rico, he stood at attention, his eyes full of condescending hatred.

The man was shaken by the boy's attitude, his arrogance. With deep regret he sent him back to the work detail, but he couldn't forget him. He'd been just a boy, a boy who'd been brainwashed well.

I appreciated such correspondence. It placed the film in a broader context for me. The Sound of Music wasn't only a story about love and family and togetherness. It was also the story of two young people, Rolf and Liesl, whose love for each other was destroyed by the Nazi war machine.

As I read the man's letter, I couldn't help reflecting that one reason Hitler and his henchmen were able to succeed in taking over Austria was that they influenced the most vulnerable members of that society: the children. This is a lesson we can never afford to forget.

ROLF

W hen we began filming, there was still one key character that had not been cast: the role of Rolf. In their casting notes, Bob and Saul envisioned Rolf as a young man, '17 going on 18. He *must Dance*. He must be likeable at the beginning and still convincing as the misled Nazi. It is one of our most demanding roles.'

Initially, Bob and Saul had simply been seeking a blond-haired seventeen-year-old who could act. A twenty-year-old named Daniel Truhitte attended the first cattle call, but he had brown hair. After less than ten seconds with the casting director, he was dismissed.

'I was in the middle of this long line of guys, all blond, all very Aryan-looking,' Dan recalls. 'I knew I didn't have a chance.'

Many weeks later, Dan's agent happened to talk to Pamela Danova, *The Sound of Music*'s dialogue coach, and learned that the role of Rolf still had not been filled. Dozens of young men had tried out – including television notables Paul Petersen (Jeff on 'The Donna Reed Show') and Bobby Diamond (Joey Newton on 'Fury'), both of whom were viewed as 'too American' for the part. The agent told Pam about a talented young man he represented who'd been passed over simply because he was a brunet. Pam called Bob Wise, and just two days later Dan was reading the cemetery scene for Bob and Saul, and dancing for Marc and Dee Dee.

They decided to give Dan a 'personality' test. He was fitted into a costume, and his hair sprayed blond. Then Bob put him on camera and began asking Dan questions, just to get a sense of him on film. After a minute of this, Dan said, 'Hey, Bob, can I sing for you?'

Up to this point, no one had even asked Dan if he *could* sing. Bob said, 'Fine. What do you want to do?'

'How about "Sixteen Going on Seventeen"?'

Bob seemed surprised, but he nodded. 'Go ahead.'

Dan remembers the moment: 'I'll never forget it. I sang the whole song, and when I was done, everyone in that room was smiling, and I knew they were going to give me a chance.'

Dan's very first appearance on camera was the most critical for him: the moment in the cemetery when Rolf blows the whistle on the von Trapps. 'I felt if I didn't do well I'd be out the door. They'd still have time to replace me.' He was a stage actor, so working in front of the cameras was a new experience for him. 'I was nervous, trying to anticipate what they wanted from me. I knew that the moment when the Captain took the gun away from Rolf was key. I felt there needed to be almost a schizophrenic shift, as Rolf went from being a normal young man to being a brainwashed young Brownshirt in a split second. I did it the best I could, and later Reggie Callow, the assistant director, took me aside and told me I had nothing to worry about. I was thrilled.'

Knowing his most difficult work was behind him, Dan settled in to enjoy the experience of making the movie, frequently visiting the sets even when he wasn't in a scene. The first day of shooting on location, when we were filming the wedding in the church in Mondsee, he came along to watch. While the technicians ran around setting up the scene, stand-ins were used to check the lighting, and Dan looked up at the altar and saw my German stand-in, Gabriele.

'There was this beautiful girl,' he remembers. 'I had to find out who she was, and I asked one of the translators. He told me her name and said she couldn't speak any English. I spent the entire morning saying some very flattering comments to her in English, only to find out at lunch that she spoke it fluently.' By an odd coincidence, Gabriele's parents' names were Liesl and Rolf. Dan dated her the entire time we were in Salzburg, and after two years of writing letters back and forth, they were married.

Dan and I spent hours practicing the dance in the gazebo. We rehearsed to the playback recording of the song, and there were warning clicks placed on the sound track to help us keep everything in sync: our movements, our singing, our gestures. If anything was off by a fraction of a second, it wouldn't look right on film.

Dan was fabulous to dance with, very accomplished, very professional. I loved working with him. 'I'll never forget when you fell in the gazebo,' he says. 'They had so many problems setting up that scene: the lighting was difficult, and the panes of glass leaked, there was water on the floor. I always thought that the water contributed to your slipping through the glass. It was so unexpected when it happened. The playback kept playing and you were lying there in all that glass, with everyone around you frozen in shock. It just seemed unreal.'

Even though Dan and I had a relationship on screen, and double-dated while we were in Salzburg, after we completed filming in 1964 we lost touch with each other. In 1996, I was at the premiere of an A&E film on the Rodgers and Hammerstein movie musicals in which I hosted a segment. This man with brown hair came up to me, grinning, and said, 'Hi, Charmy.' I didn't recognize him, so he tried again. 'It's Dan.'

'Oh my God.' I hadn't seen him in more than thirty years. It was so much fun to get reacquainted. Dan recalled incidents from our days in Salzburg that I'd long forgotten. 'Remember the scene where I threw pebbles at the window at the back of the house, and a maid inside the house had no idea what was going on, and right in the middle of the take she opens up the window and says, "Vat do you vant?" And then, as we shot another take, I hit the window too hard and broke the glass. And remember when they were shooting the scene where Chris and Richard [Haydn] and Nicholas are pushing the car out of the driveway. And that old car was so heavy they could barely budge it. Bob ended up having members of the crew pulling the car with ropes off camera.'

Kym and Debbie were at the A&E event, too, as was Robert Wise, and we all had a good time together. Before the evening was out, I invited Dan and his third wife, T.J., to stay with me at my house. Over the next couple of days we tried to catch up on each other's lives. It's a strange feeling to realize how quickly time slides past. It gave me pause to ask the question, 'So, Dan, what have you been doing for the last three decades?'

He told me about his work on the cabaret circuit, pairing up with dancers like Juliet Prowse, and how he'd portrayed Gene Kelly on stage at the MGM Grand in Las Vegas. It was fun to learn that he'd played Captain von Trapp on stage in North Carolina, and that 'Entertainment Tonight' actually covered his performance on the night of his fiftieth birthday. More recently, he has been taking special tour groups to the sites in and around Salzburg where we filmed the movie.

'I've been amazed at the following I've had from being Rolf,' Dan says. 'If I could have played only one role in my life, I've done it. I feel so blessed to have been Rolf. *The Sound of Music* made my work immortal, made us immortal. Our dance in the gazebo will be here long after we're both gone. I'll be forever grateful for that.'

Still, he sometimes wishes Rolf were more of a good guy. 'You know, in the original play, Rolf doesn't turn the von Trapps in. Yet in the film, for dramatic purposes, Rolf blows the whistle, knowing that he could have been sending Liesl and her family to their deaths.

'If I could, I'd rewrite the script. I'd give it a totally different ending. In my version, when the Nazis discover that the nuns have pulled out the distributor caps and spark plugs, they return to the abbey and are going to execute them. Rolf arrives in the nick of time and shoots all the lousy Nazis, and becomes a hero.' Dan grins. 'I think that's a much better ending.'

*D*ear Nicky,
   I'm thinking of writing down some of my memories about making The Sound of Music. *What are some of your favorites? Can I share them?*

Love,
Charmy

Dear Charmy,
   I remember standing at the top of the stairs at the altar of the church in Mondsee with you looking so beautiful as the Maid of Honor, and thinking how perfect it all was, and how proud I felt, and how someday I wanted to be married just like this, and to someone just like you.
   I was always a little bit in awe of you because you seemed to do it all so effortlessly, the singing and the dancing, and for me, a gawky fourteen-year-old, it was all very difficult. I always loved any moment I got to share with you on screen because it wasn't like being considered just one of the children, it was being considered a real actor, a real grown-up actor. I wanted to be with the professionals, and be treated seriously, like you were. So I loved the chance to dance with you, because it was a genuine screen moment, which I knew was then followed by Julie and Chris doing

the Laendler. Despite my terror of dancing, and knowing I wasn't much good, it didn't matter because I was with you. Interesting today how many people mention that as one of the most charming moments in the film. I've always wanted to be given a second chance at that dance, to wear Chris's tie and tails and white gloves and dance with you properly, not as brother and sister.

I remember that time we were up at Werfen to shoot the opening of 'Do-Re-Mi' and it rained for hours, and you and I and Saul and Betty were in a cow shed waiting for the sky to clear, and we all were talking and laughing and Saul was telling stories about musicals and joking about the hard roll and cheese we had for breakfast, and I remember your laughter, and I just thought, I don't want this rain to ever stop. I just love this and these people and this world.

I still do.

Love,
Nicky

NICKY

I n his own words, Nicholas Hammond was like a huge German-shepherd puppy in 1964. The very first thing I remember about him was his smile. He was so enthusiastic, so passionate. I loved being around him, right from the very moment we met.

He was always surprised that he was cast as Friedrich. When he showed up for his interview in New York, he had just been injured in a skiing accident. There were dozens and dozens of other children being interviewed for the different parts, and he could pick out all the potential Friedrichs: the young teenage boys with blond hair. There Nicky was, with dark-brown hair, his arm in a sling, and his two front teeth missing. He was astounded when Twentieth Century Fox signed him for the part.

I'm sure he was chosen because he was quite a talented young actor. Angela Cartwright also had a great deal of experience. At the age of four, she played Paul Newman's daughter in *Somebody Up There Likes Me* (directed by Bob Wise). She was the most recognized among us, having been Danny Thomas's daughter in 'Make Room for Daddy' for several years. The other children also had acting credits to their name. Debbie Turner had made dozens of commercials. Kym Karath had appeared in three films, including *Spencer's Mountain* with Henry Fonda. And Nicholas Hammond came in the door with *Lord of the Flies* on his résumé, as well as several Broadway plays. The kid could act.

Nicholas has always joked that most people get to go through puberty in private but he had to do it in front of 350 million people. Of course, it truly was his choice. Even at that young age, Nicky knew exactly what he wanted to do with his life: he wanted to act on the stage and screen. He has succeeded at doing that nonstop for almost forty years.

For me, he was an inspiration during the days we worked together. He was always upbeat, always very professional, and very dedicated to doing his best in every take. I felt an instant bond with him, and then our mothers became friends. Eventually, Nicky and his mother rented an apartment near our home, so I saw him constantly.

Over the years, he has become one of my closest confidants. I absolutely adore him. Initially, of course, our relationship was one between an adult and a child. But then, as he got older, that began to change. We became equals. I remember the very day it happened.

He was in the middle of his freshman year at Princeton. I was in New York on business and took the train out to see him. I had no idea how important this visit would be to Nicky. He was away from home, and in an Ivy League school where he was very much the low man on the totem pole. He tells the story vividly.

'There were no girls on the Princeton campus at that time; it was still an all-male school. The only women I ever saw during the week were the staff housecleaners who took care of the dormitories. I was a freshman, the lowest life form on campus, a paramecium among plebes, and at times very lonely. And then you came to visit.

'You were wearing that exquisite champagne mink coat that you'd bought with the money you earned on the film. That coat wouldn't be very politically correct now, but it was stunning to see you in it when you arrived. You were like a princess. And you were there to see *me*.

'I took you to the dining hall for dinner. Inside those Gothic stone walls were hundreds of young men seated at heavy rectory tables, eating supper. I'll never forget it. As I walked you down the center aisle on my arm, every fork stopped in mid-air, every head froze and followed us, and the place was silent.

'We got our food and found a place to sit. And the buzz started. I could hear them talking, even as I listened to you. All their eyes were on you, stealing glimpses. All of them were wondering, How come the squirt freshman has got a girl like *that*?

'In those days, pretty girls would get spooned, which meant, as you walked out of the room, this hormonal soup of young men would bang their spoons upon their tables, sort of like a round of applause. I'd seen a handful of girls go through this, but I'd never witnessed anything like what happened as we walked out. It wasn't just that every spoon in the entire hall was banging on the tables. Some of the guys had raced into the kitchen and gotten lids to pans, anything they could find to make noise. We exited amid a cacophony of admiration and lust for you, which understandably did my freshman ego a world of good.

'To me, your visit reconnected me with my other life, the professional life I hoped would continue after I graduated. There I was, leading a scholarly life amid the wilds of New Jersey, yet seeing you reminded me of this other world I belonged to.

'We walked into the chapel on campus and I realized that it was the first time we'd been in a church together since we filmed Maria's wedding in Mondsee, Austria. But something had happened, something had changed. I was no longer this boy; I was becoming a man. And, standing there in that chapel, I felt for the first time I was dealing with you as a grown-up. Outside of the inconvenience of you having a husband, I allowed the thought of "us" to enter my freshman mind.

'Of course, the next day everything turned back into pumpkins and mice. But for one day, in the wasteland of New Jersey, a princess had visited our campus – had visited me. That one day got me through that whole year, and I think the next as well.'

It was delightful to see Nicky there at Princeton, suddenly all grown up. I knew, by the way he held my arm, that he was glad to have an old friend in residence, even if only for a short time. And on that day I realized that the dynamics between us had changed. Nicky wasn't just a member of my *Sound of Music* family – he was also a lifelong best friend.

Nicholas Hammond is one of the gifts *The Sound of Music* gave to me. Our relationship is very precious. Nicky is the brother I never had. Actually, maybe he's better than a real brother. We avoided all the sibling rivalry and got down to the good stuff. Of all the people I know on the planet, he is one of the few I can call on in a crisis. He knows everything about me – and still likes me anyway. He has been there for me during every difficult period of my life: after my divorce, after deaths in my family, during career difficulties. And I hope I have been there for him. Nights when we can sit in front of a fireplace and share a bottle of wine and reminisce are as good as it gets.

I helped teach him to water-ski on one ski. He was a natural, learning so quickly that by the end of the first day he was skiing wonderfully. I teased him later in the boat: 'You might not be able to dance, Nicky, but you've got good balance.'

Nicky grinned at me. 'These two left feet work beautifully on one ski.'

My little brother 'Friedrich.' We were put together as fictional brother and sister and, somewhere along the way, became real ones. Nicky is my brother, and more – he is my friend.

*O*ver the years, all of us involved in the film have promoted it around the world through interviews with newspapers and magazines and radio and television stations. Generally, we get asked very similar questions: What are our favorite song and scene? What have we been doing since the movie was made? What's Julie Andrews like? But every once in a while, we get caught off guard, like during an interview Nicky and I had with Martin and Molloy, a pair of radio talk-show hosts in Australia. Here's only a brief sampling of their 'interview.'

Martin: Our guests today are two of those von Trapp kiddies. Charmian Carr and Nicholas Hammond.

Molloy: Have we locked the doors?

Martin: Ja!

Molloy: (German accent) Excellent! We have these von Trapp children right where we want them!

Me: Oh my . . .

Nicky: I should have warned you about these two.

Martin: I was reading the other day. You know, The Sound of Music has fans all around the world. And you find them in the most unexpected places. The Unabomber. The

268

Sound of Music *is apparently one of the few films that he'll watch, and I'm thinking, Well, it must be all those brown paper packages tied up with string.*

Molloy: *Have you seen his hut in the hills of Montana? It's alive – with the sound of explosives.*

Me: *(No sound, just staring at the two of them with my mouth hanging wide open.)*

Martin: *It's just good to see you in long pants, Nicholas.*

Nicky: *Well, yes, I think we're all grateful for that.*

Martin: *Tell us about your interior-design work, Charmian. You worked for Michael Jackson, I see.*

Me: *(nodding cautiously) I'm not sure I want to go there.*

Nicky: *I don't think you should go there at all. Time for a little brotherly advice . . . (After twenty more minutes of this . . .)*

Martin: *Well, thanks for talking to us today. Now we'll let you run out of this studio as we release the hounds. Let's see how fast these von Trapp kiddies can run.*

Nicky: *And you never even asked us what Julie Andrews was like.*

Martin and Molloy: *That's a whole 'nother show.*

JULIE

'What's Julie Andrews like?' Even now, all these years after the film's release, it is one of the first questions I get asked in interviews. This question is both easy and hard to answer.

When we were working on the film, in between takes it wasn't unusual for Julie to sing us the 'Indian Love Call' – slightly off key. The entire crew would break into hysterics. The next minute, she'd get the kids giggling by looking at them cross-eyed. Such antics weren't attempts to be the center of attention. Julie was absolutely focused upon the task at hand, committed to making the film the best it could be. To her, that meant not only doing her best performance on camera, but also helping in any way she could to support the work of the others involved.

One day, after we'd been in Salzburg for many weeks, she took the entire crew and some of the cast to the ballet in Munich. Her invitation requested that we bring passports and spare handkerchiefs (clean), and that we not speak to the driver (he would be drunk), and was signed 'Julie Andrews, Bus Mother.' She rented a bus and off we went, singing and telling jokes all the way to Munich, and all the way back. This was paid for out of Julie's own pocket, and was her lovely nod to acknowledge the efforts of all the men and women working behind the scenes to make the film a success.

Such gestures made us all want to stay her chums when the production was over. But though close relationships happened between many of us, Julie chose to move on. I don't know why. To me, that's her business. I do know that *The Sound of Music* was the third film she did in one single year (on the heels of *Mary Poppins* and *The Americanization of Emily*), and that she made it while parenting a very young child. She had a lot on her plate, and it had all happened very quickly.

Of course, Julie had been a star on Broadway for years, and she had also worked on television. Her very first special with Carol Burnett had aired in 1962; ironically, one of the skits they did was a spoof of *The Sound of Music* entitled 'The Pratt Family' featuring a large Swiss family singing two songs. 'The Things We Like Best' pokes fun at 'My Favorite Things' by enumerating such favorites as 'pigs' feet and cheese.' In 'Sounds for Everything,' which parodies 'Do-Re-Mi' with lyrics like 'ding-dong, yum-yum, and ho-ho-ho,' Carol Burnett belts out, 'You all can sing along if it doesn't make you sick!'

At that time, Julie probably had no inkling that she herself would one day play the role of Maria von Trapp on film – nor any notion of how famous she would become or the cost it would carry for her.

It wasn't just *The Sound of Music* that rocketed her career skyward. *Mary Poppins* premiered in August of 1964, just as we were finishing principal photography. Then *The Americanization of Emily* was released in November. Although it's inaccurate to say Julie Andrews was an instant success (she had, after all, been performing since childhood), she *did* become, quite suddenly, a global phenomenon.

The shift from Broadway star to international film superstar had to have knocked her askew. She was mobbed in public, and even on a secluded beach couldn't claim a moment alone with her daughter without being hounded by fans. Perhaps even worse, her career became compartmentalized. Audiences and critics alike wanted to see her only in 'Maria-type' roles.

So, although immediately following the film's release Julie did make an effort to stay in touch with everyone, and even had all the kids over to her house for a swim party, as time went by, and she became more and more hounded by the outside world, she became more private.

I was in touch with her off and on in the days following the premiere. Before I left on my promotional tour, Julie counseled me on how to use the money I made from the picture. 'Buy a mink, Charmy,' she said. 'You'll own it forever, and it'll always remind you of how you came to have it.' It was not controversial to wear fur coats back then; in fact, Julie had a gorgeous mink with her in Salzburg. Bob Wise has a very fond memory of that mink.

The last scene they shot in Austria was part of the first scene in the movie, when Maria is up on the mountaintop, singing. The location where they were filming was inaccessible by car. So all the equipment and cast and crew were transported to the site in wagons pulled by teams of oxen. One of Bob's favorite moments was when Julie Andrews arrived by oxcart, in that rain-soaked Austrian meadow, wearing her exquisite mink coat to try to stay warm.

So the first and only purchase I made with my money from Fox was a champagne-colored mink coat at a store in Beverly Hills recommended by Julie. She was right. I have it to this day, and it always reminds me of *The Sound of Music*.

Bob also tells another, more revealing story about Julie during that last shoot. To get that first shot of her in the meadow, they strapped a cameraman to the side of a helicopter that swooped down over the field. It was a very difficult shot, because the timing of her spin had to be perfect. The helicopter made so much noise that Marc Breaux had to cue her with a bullhorn to begin her spin. The chopper whisked down toward her just above the meadow – and Julie would be blown completely off her feet by the wind coming off its blades as the helicopter circled past. That's how close to her the camera needed to be. It took them ten takes, and after each one, Julie

Andrews lifted herself off the ground, ready to spin again.

Though we didn't cross paths often after the film was released, Julie helped me when I was in a jam over my contract with Fox. I called her out of total frustration. I was stuck. I had signed a seven-year contract with the studio, but they weren't using me on any projects, nor would they release me to work elsewhere. In fact, when I was up for the television series 'Peyton Place,' Bob Wise himself prevented me from working in it. He didn't want 'Liesl' to have a tainted image.

Julie was more than willing to help me out. She linked me up with her agent, and he was ultimately able to get me out of my contract. Of course, shortly afterward, I married and stopped acting in films altogether. But I always appreciated Julie's assistance, and always felt she'd be there for me if I needed her in any professional capacity.

I have seen her only rarely in the years since. The last time was at the film's twenty-fifth anniversary celebration. She was, as always, polite and cordial.

'What's Julie Andrews like?' people ask. 'Is she like Maria? Are you close friends?' I see the hope in their eyes that somehow the relationship we had on camera has been sustained all these years. I don't want to disappoint them, to break the illusion, but the truth is, we don't have a personal relationship.

What's Julie like? She's a pro. In 1964, she

immersed herself in the role of a novice nun who falls in love and becomes the mother to seven children. Throughout the entire picture she's acting, but certain parts of her personality are there, unmasked, on screen: her sense of humor, her intelligence, her English propriety.

There's an old adage: the camera doesn't lie. The magic up on the screen is real. Julie Andrews is largely responsible for creating it. Just because a lifelong friendship didn't result between us doesn't discount what *The Sound of Music* means to me. For Julie Andrews didn't go to Salzburg to make friends; she went there to make a movie. And she made a great one.

I receive letters from fans many years after they first saw the film, telling me the impact the film had on them. This one from a young actor affected me deeply.

'I grew up a fish out of water in Brooklyn. While other kids were playing stickball, I was learning to play the piano. When I was seven, my father was working full-time while my mother was studying for her master's, and there were times when I felt ignored. One rainy Saturday, I was crying because it seemed to me that my mom always had to work, and I wanted her to pay attention to me. That day, she put aside her work and took me to the movies. It was an afternoon that would change my life.

'I had only been to a movie theater once before. I had seen The Wizard of Oz, *but had run out screaming when the Wicked Witch of the West appeared. This time, we were to see the rerelease of a film called* The Sound of Music.

'The minute the overture started, I was entranced. When Liesl and Rolf danced in the gazebo, I was mesmerized. Later, when Rolf sides with the Nazis, I could see the disappointment in Liesl's face, and I got a lump in my throat. I felt as though I'd been transported to another place and time. As I walked out of the theater, I squinted as if waking up from a dream. As my mother drove me home on the Long

Island Expressway, it was still pouring, and I looked out my window at the drops of rain and relived that gazebo scene in my mind, over and over. And I knew, even though I was only seven, I knew: I was going to be an actor when I grew up.

'I'll never forget when you accepted my invitation to come and see me in my first West Coast musical. It was a powerful moment, twenty-five years after the fact, for me to be able to thank you in person for inspiring me as a small child. The Sound of Music *– and you – changed my life. You are the reason I am here on this stage.'*

THE FINAL CURTAIN

The old projector clicks rhythmically as the black-and-white images flicker on the screen set up in the living room. Before my eyes, my mother and her brother Edward as young children are dancing on a vaudeville stage. They age rapidly, becoming teenagers in the next moment, then adults. Interspersed between clips of them dancing are shots of their names up in lights on theater marquees. They are never on top, but still, they are in lights, 'The Oehmen Twins,' though they were not really twins at all. In evening clothes, they spin rapidly across the stage, the film speed too fast, making their graceful movements look almost comical. Edward tosses my mother over his back and tries to carry her off stage, only to return.

It's fun to watch them. It gives me nothing but good feelings. I wish I could hear the music, the words that they are saying to each other. Mother finally feigns punching her brother in the jaw, flips Edward over *her* back, and carries him off stage. Then they race back out, waving at the audience, laughing, and my mother winks at the camera. This is Rita Oehmen at her best.

My mother was happy then. She loved to perform. She was someone other people liked to be around. She hadn't become bitter yet, or let alcohol dominate her life.

She started drinking when she was a teenager. She'd have a glass of something before she went on stage to calm her nerves. It wasn't until much later that she went on binges. Her own mother was an alcoholic, so it was in the genes, but I don't like to think that her fate was inevitable.

Mom was born and raised in Chicago and was five when she was first pushed out on stage by her mother. She was paired with her eight-year-old brother, Edward, and they were billed as 'The Oehmen Twins' because they were the same size and twins had audience appeal.

Throughout her entire childhood, my mother performed at least four or five times a day, singing and dancing. I can only imagine what impact this life-style had upon her and her self-image. Maybe it planted the seeds that would later bear the fruit of her bitterness. All I know is, the only time my mother was truly happy was when she was up there in front of an audience. To be a star, to thrill a crowd or make them laugh, was something she needed the way she needed air to breathe.

Mom did the vaudeville act with Edward until she was twenty and branched out on her own, doing a nightclub show that incorporated singing and dancing with stand-up comedy. During this time, she also attended two colleges simultaneously, going to school during the day and working hotel and club dates at night, until she earned her degree in theater arts. I don't know when she ever had a chance to sleep.

She performed her musical-comedy act at big hotels around the country. She seemed on a trajectory for a hugely successful career. Entertainment magazines touted her as 'the nation's newest and most versatile comedienne of song.' In 1937, while she was appearing at the Biltmore in Los Angeles, she was discovered by talent scouts. Three studios expressed interest in hiring her, and she chose the one with initials that matched her own: RKO (for Rita Kathleen Oehmen). The head of RKO was planning on replacing Ginger Rogers, and pairing my mom with Fred Astaire, but in a screen test, Mom looked too young. Fred told her, 'I love you, Rita, but I can't have a leading lady who looks like my granddaughter.'

It's ironic. The same youthful looks that thwarted my mother's big chance in films helped me secure the role of Liesl when I was twenty-one.

RKO instead cast her opposite George O'Brien in a Western, *Gunlaw*. It wasn't very memorable, but it used to run on television and my sisters and I always thought it was a riot to watch because of Mom's heavy makeup and outrageous hairdo, not very believable on a woman in the Wild West.

After two years in Hollywood, and only one more film, a Lucille Ball picture in which she had a bit part, Mom returned to her work on the live stage. She met my father in Canada at a nightclub where he played in the pit orchestra that accompanied her in a show. I don't recall their talking much about their first meeting or how they fell in love. I know that he took her bowling, and then out to dinner, and that after she left the next week, they corresponded for a year before deciding to get married.

They lived in Toronto until my sister Sharon was born. Then my mother wanted to go back home to Chicago. World War II was raging, and my father enlisted in the Canadian Allied Expeditionary Forces Band with his brother. He was able to stay home for only a short time after my arrival on December 27, 1942.

My mother always told me mine was a horrible birth. I was a breech – I came into the world feet-first. Personally, I think I was just bracing myself for what was to come.

It was my father who named me Charmian. A friend of his had a sister by that name and Dad always loved the sound: *Shar*-mee-an. I wasn't always fond of it when I was growing up. Everyone always mispronounced it, calling me Char-*mane*, as if I were some kind of dish at a Chinese restaurant. For a long time, I just wanted to be plain Jane. But I've grown more fond of it over the years. It comes from Shakespeare's play *Antony and Cleopatra*. Charmian was Cleopatra's attendant, a care-giver in a supporting role. My father gave me a name that defined me quite well.

The week I was born, the cover of *Life* magazine featured a lonely housewife smoking a cigarette and staring off into space. I look at that picture and it makes me think of Rita, my mother, all alone in

Chicago with two little babies, without an audience or even a husband to give her applause at the end of a long day. By the time I was six months old, she'd returned to the stage, touring the country off and on for several years, including two tours with Victor Borge. Ironically, Victor Borge would later be seriously considered for the role of Uncle Max in the film of *The Sound of Music*. But he wanted the character to be made much stronger, which would have required additional scenes. Bob Wise felt the script was already pushing the limits in terms of length, so Victor Borge was ultimately ruled out.

After Darleen was born, Mom stayed closer to home, doing one-night concerts and summer stock. In 1948, she was named 'The Loveliest Mother in Chicago' and in an interview said, 'Training children to be individuals is the most important job of all parents.'

I know Mom loved us. I know she was glad to have her daughters. But sometimes I felt we'd never be enough. The only way we seemed to make her happy was by getting an ovation. Vicariously, our performances seemed to sustain her – for a while. But when my sisters and I grew up and began to be successful on our own, Mom became more and more frustrated by what she viewed as her own failed career. The fact that she'd had a career on the stage and in movies didn't satisfy her. Rather than be proud of what she'd accomplished, she chose to become bitter about what had passed her by. Mom, who had always been our cheer-leader, began to tear us down. She would say it was our fault her career had ended. We were the reason she'd been forced to quit acting. She viewed our success with jealousy, not pride.

When Darleen landed a lead role on the television series 'Miss Winslow and Son,' we all went to the taping of the premiere. After the final act, the producer came over to where we were sitting and introduced our family to the two hundred other people in the audience. Then he said to Mom, 'You must be very proud of your daughter Darleen. Didn't she do just great!'

Mom paused, and I closed my eyes. I knew what was coming. I'd heard it before. 'Great? Why, I've got more talent in my little finger than she's got in her whole body!' The poor producer stood there stunned, mumbled a quick thanks, and moved back to the stage.

On an afternoon in October of 1995, my phone rang. It was Sharon. 'I just got the call we've been waiting for,' she said. I knew right away what my sister meant: Mom was dead.

I hadn't seen her in two years, even though she lived only a short drive away. It had been a 'tough-love' decision by all three of us girls, a last-ditch effort to get Mom to save herself before the drinking killed her. We told her, 'We love you. We'll always be here for you. But we're not going to communicate with you unless you stop drinking.' We believed that, if she loved us enough, by turning our backs on her we would inspire her to change. It didn't work. And now she was gone.

After years of binge drinking, my mother's esophagus had ruptured. She bled to death, alone, in her own house. The coroner told me it wasn't a painful way to die. 'You can't breathe,' he said. 'It's over fast.'

I cried for our mother, for what might have been. When she was sober, Mom was so funny, so full of life. After I got divorced, she signed us up for a line-dancing class. She was over seventy, yet she could still do the high kicks, the graceful moves. She was the most talented woman I ever knew, and as I sat with my sisters on that day when her body was found, I couldn't help feeling both angry and sad about what had been lost – not just to Mom, but to all of us.

During her life, our mother had so many people to love, who loved her. She had three daughters and five grandchildren and dozens of friends. But all she could see were her failures. With her lens distorted by alcohol, she could only see what she didn't have. But it could have been so different. It *should* have been so different.

At Mom's funeral, people were given an opportunity to say a few words about her. I got up to say how much I felt she had spurred me on to accomplish great things. Her way of encouraging me wasn't always the best. But she had given me a love of music and dance, and an independence that has always served me well.

Other friends talked about how her alcoholism had pulled her down, how tragic the disease can be. But then Nicky got up. I'll always be grateful that Nicholas Hammond happened to be in town. By then, he was living in Australia, and was Stateside infrequently. By sheer coincidence, he was in Los Angeles the week that Mom died. I'll never forget his words at her funeral.

'I have known Rita Farnon since I was thirteen,' he said. 'She was the life of the party. She could be so funny. She had this enormous talent, yet she didn't know where to channel it sometimes. She hurt people. But if you go and see the Sistine Chapel, you don't lean back and look at that incredible piece of artwork and wonder what kind of a person Michelangelo was. You don't think about whether he suffered from depression or a proclivity to drink. You stand in awe of his legacy. And that is what I am doing today.

'Look at her three daughters. They are Rita Farnon's gift to the world. Rita raised them as a single mother. All of them are standing tall on their own, leading amazing lives. Those of us who are lucky enough to know Sharon and Charmy and Darleen should be down on our knees today thanking God for giving us Rita. Her daughters are her master-piece. To me, they are a legacy as beautiful as the Sistine Chapel.'

Mom always wanted to live by the ocean, so we took her ashes to a private beach up the coast and scattered our mother's remains to the wind. As we

290

stood on the bluff overlooking the Pacific, three porpoises appeared just beyond the waves, as if representing the three of us she'd left behind, and I thought about Nicky's words.

I watch the old home movie of Mom in vaudeville now when I want to remember her. She is happy up there on the stage. I wish she could have been just as happy out of the lights and down in the real world with those of us who loved her.

In the final moments of the old film, the lights on the stage become so bright it is hard to see my mother's face on the screen anymore. She is a silhouette, fading, becoming dimmer and dimmer as the lights get ever brighter, until suddenly the film ends and clicks off the reel, flapping wildly. I reach over and turn the projector off and the screen stares at me blankly. The stage has disappeared – and so has my mother.

*T*he film is such a great love story and seems to touch so many people. This story from a woman who served overseas as a captain in World War II touched my own heart.

'Romance is something that I've never experienced in my life. It's sad, because at heart I am such a romantic. I always hoped for deep love, but I got skipped over somehow. There was the Depression, and then the war, and life just had hard edges. Romance, or the chance for it, just passed me by. So here I am, eighty-three years old, and still waiting.

'To me The Sound of Music *is the most romantic movie ever made. I'm like a dreamy kid when I watch it. I'll put the video on three or four times a year, and it always picks me up when I'm feeling low. It awakens my heart.*

'I think I would swoon if someone were to put their arms around me and hold me as the Captain does Maria. It's never happened. Still, even though it hasn't, the movie makes me feel as if I know how such a romantic encounter would feel. When Maria and the Captain realize they are in love as they dance at the party, and later, when they admit it to each other in the gazebo, those scenes satisfy a need in me.

'If I had been blind from birth, and suddenly had sight, and saw the color red, even if it was just for an instant, I would always know what red looks like.

The movie has done that for me. I believe I know what love, real romantic love, would feel like. The Sound of Music *taught me the color of love.'*

BOB AND SAUL

Robert Wise and Saul Chaplin both hold a special place in my heart. Like my siblings from the film, I consider these men to be part of my second family.

Robert Wise is a legend. He has won four Oscars, the National Medal for the Arts, and the Lifetime Achievement Award from the American Film Institute. I feel so fortunate to have worked with him at the height of his career. Now we walk slowly together down the sidewalk to his favorite restaurant in Beverly Hills. He is eighty-five and still goes to his office every day and directs films. When we get to the restaurant, everybody knows him by name. The waitress knows his favorite dish, his favorite Cabernet. He has earned this recognition, this respect.

The Sound of Music puzzles him a bit. He shakes his head with a half-smile. 'Out of all the films I've made, it's the only one anyone wants to talk about.' It's not because Bob doesn't love the film and all of us and all the memories. It's because he also loves the other films he brought to the screen: *Executive Suite. Run Silent, Run Deep. West Side Story. The Haunting* (the original version). *The Sand Pebbles. Star! The Andromeda Strain. The Hindenburg.*

More than one reporter has asked him, 'What

makes *The Sound of Music* so successful?' One weekly magazine in the seventies devoted an entire cover article to this burning question.

'I don't know,' Bob answers. 'I wasn't trying to make a statement with it.'

Bob is the kind of person who makes his work look so effortless that it's possible to lose sight of what he's contributed. He's a genius, a perfectionist. I remember sometimes he would call for another take and I would think, 'Not again. Isn't what we have good enough?' 'Good enough' isn't in Bob Wise's vocabulary. Even the two seconds in which a frog hopped by our feet (having just been flung by Maria, who has discovered it in her pocket) required numerous takes. 'He was a very uncooperative frog,' Bob remembers. Because of his attention to detail, and his willingness to make each shot as good as possible, his films are nearly flawless.

I remember how hard he worked, how patient he was. There were times when disasters threatened, but Bob never lost his cool. Any problem had a solution. His mastery was patience.

Near the end of the filming in Austria, there was one last shot he needed to get. It was the section of the opening number in which Maria walks among birch trees along the edge of a small stream. The entire set was fabricated in a meadow. The young birch trees were planted, and a brook was created by lining a ditch with a black plastic tarp and filling it with water. But the farmer who owned the meadow was angry at these American filmmakers. Though they were paying him for the use of his field, he felt they were upsetting his cows. Using a pitchfork, he poked holes in the plastic liner of the stream. The brook disappeared, and production time was lost while it was repaired. This was all Bob needed at the time.

Dick Zanuck placed a frantic call to Austria that afternoon. With the studio on the verge of total bankruptcy, he couldn't afford one more day. Bob promised him, 'If I don't get the shot tomorrow, we'll fly home.' He had no idea what he would do if the weather didn't cooperate. The day began dark and gloomy – but then the sun broke through, just enough for Bob to get the final shot of Maria in the birch trees. 'That was one of the tightest situations I've ever been in,' he recalls.

We had a fight once. Only once. It began at the twenty-fifth anniversary of the film's release, when the seven of us who had played the von Trapp children agreed to help promote the release of the video in London. A feud ignited that wasn't resolved until two years later. At the core of our discontent was that perpetually sticky subject – money.

Over the years, we had promoted the film for the studio gratis. We frequently incurred our own expenses, as well as a loss of business income and time away from our families. When we were in London in 1990, we each began to talk about how the studio had gotten us to sign releases for the sound track back in 1964. We realized for the first time that there had been coercion. It didn't feel good to learn this. Unfortunately, at the same time, the studio reps running the events in London were also taking advantage of us. To add insult to injury, for one event the promoters had us on a set of stairs constructed to look exactly like the ones in the front hall of the Trapp Villa to sing 'So Long, Farewell.' The director, who kept calling us 'boys and girls,' wanted us to mimic our choreographed movements from the film. By then, we were in our thirties and forties and found his condescending treatment insulting.

For the first time ever, we put our foot down. We still promoted the film in London, but we agreed as a group that never again would we work without compensation. In essence, we tried to articulate that the studio and others involved in the film had shared in enormous profits. We had been promoting the film for free for a quarter-century because we truly loved having been a part of it, and enjoyed speaking on its behalf. But we no longer felt such promotion should come, in part, out of our own pockets, or at the expense of our dignity.

At first Bob didn't understand why any of us would be upset at the lack of compensation for our participation in promoting the film. He was hurt and upset when we finally said, 'No more.'

'I had always felt that you and the other children loved the picture and were proud to be part of a film that has retained such great popularity,' he wrote me. 'You revealed a lot of pent-up resentment and bitterness that has evidently built up over the years . . . While it's true I have made a lot of money from *The Sound of Music*, I think I earned it . . . I started directing in 1943 and in the decade of the fifties I worked very hard . . . While it's true you got the lowest salaries . . . you'll have to remember that none of you was established . . .'

All of us felt Bob deserved every dime he made from the film. But we wanted him to try to stand in our shoes. What happens if the biggest success in your life comes at the beginning, rather than the middle or the end? What if you continue to nurture that success, without compensation, and even sometimes at your own expense?

We each tried to explain our frustrations. We all assured Bob that he meant a great deal to us. We had the utmost respect for him, and our memories and experiences of our association with the film were all positive. We just wanted to be treated fairly.

Ultimately, it got resolved like any family squabble. We all had a chance to say our piece. It worked out. Future promotion would be compensated. Our relationship to one another remained the most important thing to each of us.

Many of the films Bob has left his imprint on, either as director or as editor, are among the best films ever made. The American Film Institute recently named *Citizen Kane* the number-one film of the century. Orson Welles is the complicated mastermind everyone associates with the film, but Robert Wise cut it. He's the editor. It is his rhythm, his instinct, his feel for the moment, that takes us through the labyrinth of Kane's life.

That is Bob to me. We see things through his eyes – yet his artistry is invisible, because he invites us to become immersed in the story on the screen. He is a brilliant man, a man who changed my life through his patience and guidance.

And then there was Saul Chaplin. Behind the scenes, Saul helped in so many important ways to bring magic to *The Sound of Music*. From his assistance in every aspect of the creative process to his joyous encouragement of our young cast, his imprint on *The Sound of Music* is indelible. Everybody involved in the film loved him. Heather recently commented, 'Saul was the shining light through the whole production. He was the cheerleader who kept us all going, who made us enthusiastic, who made us care. He loved everybody – and part of the love that's evident in the film is Solly up there. What a tremendous life force he was!'

Like Bob Wise, Saul Chaplin left large footprints in the history of American cinema. He wore many hats as a songwriter, vocal arranger, music director, and producer. His forty-two films include *An American in Paris, On the Town, The Jolson Story, Kiss Me Kate, Seven Brides for Seven Brothers, High*

Society, *West Side Story*, and *That's Entertainment, Part II.*

Saul's marriage to Betty Levin was one of those storybook unions in which two people in the second half of their lives discover their soul mates. As Saul himself said, it was like being in an operetta when they fell in love making *The Sound of Music*.

After nearly thirty years of marriage, Saul became very ill. For months Betty rarely left his side. When Saul died in November 1997, I thought it must have been a relief for her, but it wasn't. She was devastated at losing him. She loved taking care of Saul. She loved him. 'Solly didn't have a pretentious bone in him,' she says. 'He was the most incredible man I've ever known. He was so talented, but without any ego. He did all these fabulous things in his life. Anyone who's a fan of American musicals would recognize so much of his work, and yet they've probably never heard his name. He didn't care if anyone knew who he was. He only cared if he touched people with his music. And he did – he did his whole life.'

None of us who knew him could imagine the world without Saul Chaplin. Yet, though he's gone, his music, and his movies, live on. At his funeral, I knew there was only one way to say goodbye to this man who'd done so much for us all, and brought us such joy. I stood at his service, and sang for him, one last time.

There's a sad sort of clanging from the clock in the hall,
And the bells in the steeple too,
And up in the nurs'ry an absurd little bird is popping
  out to say 'coo-coo'
Regretfully they tell us, but firmly they compel us,
To say 'goodbye' to you . . .
So long, farewell, auf Wiedersehen, goodbye.
Goodbye . . . goodbye . . . goodbye.

*T*he film has a strong spiritual resonance. A Catholic priest relayed this story not just about the film, but about a subsequent journey he was inspired to make.

'The Sound of Music *was a favorite film when I was young. The hopefulness of it and the deep sense of faith and courage of the story appealed to me on many levels.*

'*So, in 1985, while visiting the St Joseph Seminary outside Salzburg, I was curious to see where the real von Trapps had lived. I had heard stories about what had happened there. After the von Trapps fled Austria, the Nazis had occupied the house, turning the family chapel into a beer hall. Heinrich Himmler, head of the Gestapo and an architect of the Holocaust, made his Austrian headquarters in Captain von Trapp's former office.*

'*There was one story in particular. Hitler would stay at the Trapp Villa, and on one of his visits, several drivers and orderlies were standing in the courtyard below the window of his room, and one of them was humming a Russian folk song. This so infuriated Hitler that he had all of the men in the courtyard shot, without bothering to learn which one had been singing. That story struck me as so ironic – that, in a home where such beautiful music had been born, humming a tune had become a death sentence.*

'*After the war ended, the villa reverted to the von*

Trapps, but they did not wish to return to it. They sold it to a Catholic order, and so there I was, forty-seven years after the von Trapps had left, entering the doors to their former home.

'The house was massive and dark. My destination was the Captain's office, which had been turned into a eucharistic chapel. Two large leatherbound doors opened into the chapel, and I stepped inside. It was a large room, simple but beautiful, with windows that looked out over the backyard, and kneelers on which to pray.

'As I knelt, I was struck by the powerful silence of that room. I prayed the Holy Rosary, and my experience that day approached the sublime. Tremendous evil had invaded that house and centered in that room, but somehow the presence of the Eucharist pointed toward the eternal. I felt the presence of the von Trapps, their strength of will, still there, embedded in those walls.

'Years after my visit to the Trapp Villa, I began to teach a course on the Holocaust at the College of Notre Dame. It was a subject not generally taught at Catholic colleges, but I felt a very strong need to communicate the history and questions that the Holocaust raises.

'I never made the connection before, but my experience in the Trapp Villa must have helped guide me. I prayed in a place where Himmler had executed plans for the "final solution." Later, I came to see the vital importance of teaching about what had happened. The von Trapps were always with me in the classroom, examples of the resilience of the human spirit, and how life continues beyond even the greatest evil.'

THE TRAPP FAMILY SINGERS

Our portrayal of the von Trapps' story was based upon real events, but it was fictionalized for dramatic purposes. I've always felt their true story was equally dramatic.

In the film, Maria arrives at the von Trapp home on the eve of the Nazi takeover of Austria. In truth, Maria arrived in 1926, twelve years before the Anschluss. There were five girls and two boys in the family, but the oldest child was not a girl named Liesl but a fifteen-year-old boy named Rupert. He was teased mercilessly by his siblings when *The Sound of Music* came out.

'Rupert, you look so good in a dress!'

'Should we call you Liesl now?'

He would shake his head and laugh. By then he was in his fifties and a doctor. Still, members of the real family must have wondered why it was necessary to change the facts. I don't know why the birth order was altered, other than that Rodgers and Hammerstein wrote a great song about a girl who was sixteen going on seventeen and wanted to use it in the show.

The oldest daughter was the shy one in the family, Agathe. She was born in 1913 and was twenty-five years old at the time of the Anschluss, not sixteen. She was followed by Maria (Louisa), Werner (Kurt), Hedwig (Brigitta), Johanna (Marta), and

Martina (Gretl). I understand why Maria's name was changed (to avoid confusion with Fraulein Maria), but not the other children, whose names were beautiful.

Other aspects of the story were altered as well. The children were quite musical before Maria's arrival, already singing three-part harmonies with their father. The Captain was not stern, but very loving, and would only use his bos'n's whistle to call the children when they were far from the house. Maria (the governess) did not fall in love with the Captain. She fell in love with the children. She grew to love the Captain, but not until after they were married. When they met, the Captain was on the verge of marrying Princess Yvonne of Austria, but he saw how much his children loved their governess, and he, too, fell in love with her.

On November 26, 1927, Maria married Georg von Trapp. The marriage occurred long before Hitler ever took over Germany, much less Austria. In fact, Georg and Maria would add two more children to the family, daughters Rosmarie and Eleanore, before they were faced with the Anschluss.

Maria had indeed been a novice at Nonnberg Abbey in Salzburg; that part was true. She had had a miserable childhood, losing both her parents when she was very young, and, though not initially a Catholic, she began attending Mass just to hear the music. She experienced a religious conversion, joined the Church, and set her sights on becoming a nun.

Against her will, she was sent to the home of Baron Georg von Trapp, a submarine commander in the Austro-Hungarian navy during World War I. The Captain's wife had been the former Agathe Whitehead, whose grandfather had invented the torpedo, and whose father helped create and run a torpedo plant that made the family quite wealthy. The way Agathe and Georg met was rather romantic. He was a rising star in the navy. Decorated at the age of eighteen for his service in the Boxer Rebellion in China, he was later given command of one of the very first submarines his navy ever put in service. The young lady who christened the boat with a bottle of champagne was Agathe Whitehead. They fell in love, married, and moved into a beautiful villa on the edge of the sea. She gave birth to seven children, children who would become a part of the history of the twentieth century.

During the war, they moved to a small town outside Salzburg. The Captain was an extraordinarily successful commander during World War I, and was beloved by his countrymen in much the same way Eisenhower was following World War II. But Austria (a German ally) lost the war, and with the armistice that followed, the Austro-Hungarian navy ceased to exist. Georg von Trapp was a captain without a ship. It was Agathe who provided him with a mooring, a harbor. They settled happily into their villa in Aigen. But in the early fall of 1922, the children caught scarlet fever. Agathe took care of them, and then she herself caught scarlet fever – and died. As Maria would later write in her autobiography, 'Half of [the Captain's] life had died with the Navy. Of the remaining half, most seemed to be buried with her.'

Agathe's part in the family's story was never included in any of the dramatizations about the von Trapp family. She is not known to fans of *The Sound of Music*. But she was a beautiful and special woman who gave birth to all seven of those children. She was, in large measure, responsible for the talented and courageous people they grew up to be. Without Agathe, there would have been no *Sound of Music*.

Another person omitted from the story was Father Franz Wasner, a priest they befriended who taught the family the fundamentals of music and the intricate harmonies that would later make them famous. The character of Max Detweiler in the film is loosely based on Father Wasner, but the real man behind the family singing group was not an apolitical impresario but a fine musician and priest.

The von Trapp family fortune had been lost during the European economic collapse of the early thirties, and it was then that the family hobby of singing together changed and became an occupational necessity. It was Father Wasner who guided the Trapp Family Singers to the high honors they received at the Salzburg Music Festival in 1936.

On the night of March 11, 1938, while celebrating the younger Agathe's twenty-fifth birthday, the von Trapps were listening to the radio in the library of their villa when the program was interrupted by the Austrian chancellor who announced, 'I am yielding to force. My Austria – God bless you.' At first the family sat there blankly, not understanding what was happening as strains of the Austrian national anthem filled the room. Not until their butler Hans came in and informed them that Austria had been invaded by Germany did it sink in.

The anthem on the radio ended, and a Prussian voice declared, 'Austria is dead! Long live the Third Reich!'

Maria would later write about how she felt that night. She said it was as though she had learned a dear friend had died. Her husband stared at the flag that had flown on his submarine and now hung above the fireplace mantel. Tears filled his eyes as he proclaimed, 'Austria, you are not dead. You will live on in our hearts!'

The Anschluss was pervasive and complete. As Nazis marched into Salzburg, members of the Gestapo supervised the ringing of bells at every church. Over the radio, it was announced that the citizens of Salzburg were ringing their grateful joy, which prompted twenty-three-year-old Werner von Trapp to jump angrily to his feet, his fists clenched.

Anger and confusion gave way to suspicion. The

family no longer knew whom they could trust. Even Hans, their butler (Franz in the movie), admitted he was a member of the Nazi Party. Singing the Austrian national anthem became punishable by death. 'Heil Hitler' was the only greeting allowed. The names of all the streets in Salzburg were changed to reflect the new regime, and red flags with black swastikas adorned every house. The teachers in the schools were replaced with new ones who would drum the party line into Austrian youth. Little Rosmarie von Trapp, the nine-year-old daughter of Maria and Georg, was told that her parents were 'nice, old-fashioned people who don't understand the new Party.' She was told not to try to get them to understand, to leave them alone, and never to mention at home what she was learning in school. Seven-year-old Eleanore refused to sing the new anthem in school; when asked why, she told her teacher that her father had said he'd put ground glass in his tea or finish his life on a dung heap before he'd ever sing that song. The teacher called Maria into the school and warned her that any similar outbursts would have to be reported.

In the middle of all the changes that spring of 1938, Maria learned she was pregnant. Since the births of Rosmarie and Eleanore, an attack of scarlet fever had severely damaged Maria's kidneys. She had already miscarried twice. A doctor advised her to abort the fetus she was carrying. But Maria, devoutly religious, refused, even though the doctor warned her she was risking her own life. He advised her that she should avoid all stress, all excitement. In the coming weeks, however, the admonition would prove impossible to heed.

In June of 1938, at a restaurant in Salzburg, the von Trapps were seated at a table right next to 'der Führer' himself and witnessed first-hand the thigh-slapping behavior of Hitler and his henchmen. Maria would later note, 'If one hadn't been so deeply impressed by the fact that this man held the fate of many millions in his fingers, one wouldn't have looked a second time at him.' She found him vulgar and crass.

On that same day, Georg received his fateful invitation to accept a post as the commander of a submarine base in the German navy. Just days later, Rupert, the oldest son, by then a doctor, received his own summons, requesting him to go to Vienna and take up a post in a Nazirun hospital. Then came the long-distance phone call from Berlin informing the family that they had been chosen to sing on the radio for the 'beloved Führer's' birthday.

In the course of a single week, the family was faced with three requests from the Third Reich, all of which they intended to decline. And they knew – they couldn't say no to Hitler three times and not be in danger.

A momentous and difficult choice was at hand. Georg put it to his children. 'Do we want to keep the material goods we still have: our home, our friends, all the things we are fond of? Then we shall have to give up the spiritual goods: our faith and our honor.'

In most people's eyes, they chose the harder path. They refused to acquiesce like so many of their countrymen. Each packed a single suitcase. It was merely a family vacation, they told everyone, some mountain climbing in South Tirol, Italy. They left their home, fleeing not by secretly hiking over the Alps, as is depicted in the film, but under the ruse of taking a brief holiday. This may have been less dramatic, but it carried the same risks and sacrifices.

Many weeks later, they arrived in America by ship. Maria, who had been warned to avoid excitement because of her pregnancy, survived with the child within her still thriving. In a hotel in New York on their first day on American soil, the family faced a cruel reality. All they had in their pockets were four American dollars. Somehow, they would have to find a way to survive. There were twelve people to feed – including Father Wasner, who had made the journey with them. Their need to survive would give birth to the Trapp Family Singers in America.

Their lives were forever changed by the choices they made. Today, we know the potential cost of their defiance of Hitler: they faced imprisonment – or worse. In leaving, they lost everything they owned, their beloved home in Aigen, their friends, their language, their cultural heritage and customs and comforts. But they retained their honor. They kept their souls.

Their adventure in America was just beginning. They were in a foreign land where they would be viewed as refugees, and where they would have to fight to remain. Maria, on arriving in America after a brief tour singing in Europe, would make a nearly disastrous mistake. When an Immigration official asked her, 'Length of stay?' she answered. 'I am so glad to be here. I never want to leave again!' The family did not have immigration papers, only visitors' visas.

Misinterpreting Maria's enthusiasm as a threat that the family might try to remain in the States illegally, Immigration detained the entire family on Ellis Island, virtually imprisoning them. If it were not for friends in New York, they might well have faced deportation, and an uncertain fate back to Europe.

On January 17, 1939, a healthy ten-pound, two-ounce baby boy was born to Maria and Georg. They named him Johannes Georg. His birth symbolized the rebirth of the entire family in America.

The Sound of Music was largely a work of fiction. But it had such a global audience that the von Trapps themselves couldn't escape its impact. As Johannes recently explained to Nicholas, 'Most people I meet just want to know who played me in the film. They don't want to hear that I was born in America in 1939.'

Nicky was perplexed by this. Johannes was a *real*

von Trapp. Wasn't that better than being merely an actor who'd portrayed one?

Johannes just smiled at him wryly. 'They want me to be you.'

'Oh.'

Perhaps the fiction of the film hit its most absurd level when, during the Reagan administration, the arrival of the Austrian ambassador in the East Room of the White House was announced by the playing of 'Edelweiss,' which someone assumed was the Austrian national anthem.

Although the real story of the Trapp Family Singers was not the same one we told in the film, I believe *The Sound of Music* captures the essence of their story. The film portrays a family bound by love and the healing power of music. As Maria von Trapp herself once wrote, 'Music is an international language which speaks from heart to heart and doesn't need the medium of a human tongue. Whether our audience was French, English, Dutch, or Italian – in our music we could talk to them across the barrier of a foreign language . . . Let us forget all quarreling in the world and be happy together . . . Music – what a powerful instrument, what a mighty weapon.'

*M*arty is almost ninety, but she remembers quite clearly an event that happened sixty years ago.

'We read about them in an article in the Dayton paper,' she explains. 'The Trapp Family Singers. The article explained how they were struggling to get by, how they had arrived here in the States with nothing. My husband, Jim, and I weren't going to go, but then we decided we should support them. It was the end of the Depression, and people did things like that.'

She pauses, remembering. 'There were a lot of German-Americans in the Dayton area. And it was a time when one was feeling funny about being German. My own family had German-Swiss origins.

'The war was going on. We weren't in it yet, but Germany had attacked Poland and was beginning to threaten England and France. And obviously, it was because of the Germans that the von Trapps had fled Austria. It made German-Americans feel strange.'

Her eyes get a faraway look. 'That night, the NCR Auditorium in Dayton was packed. Sold out. The von Trapps were wonderful. Their singing just took my breath away. I wanted them to go on and on. But, finally, Maria, the mother, stepped up to the microphone and said that they were going to sing their last number.

'It was "Silent Night" in German, and it was the

319

most beautiful thing I'd ever heard. One by one, people in the audience began to stand up and add their voices to the von Trapps'. Many had tears in their eyes. A hateful thing was happening in Germany, but that didn't mean all Germans were evil. There was nothing but love as the room filled with the singing of that holy song.

'When the music ended, it was the most incredible thing. Nobody clapped. The hall was totally silent. The von Trapps understood. Something had happened between them and all of us in the auditorium, as if they had touched us with a healing hand. They stood for a long moment, sharing the silence with us, then they bowed deeply and walked from the stage. I've never seen anything so moving in my whole life.'

EDELWEISS

We rode on a steamy bus through horrendous traffic to the theater on Broadway. It was balmy for a December night in New York, with temperatures in the sixties. The air conditioning on the bus failed, and because the Christmas tree was being lit at Rockefeller Center, every street was in gridlock. One of the von Trapps managed to pop open the little vent in the ceiling of the bus, and we all gave him a round of applause. But there were anxious glances at our wristwatches as the minutes ticked past. It took us almost an hour to get from our hotel to the theater. We were ten minutes late for the opening curtain of *The Sound of Music*, and all of us were crestfallen.

Astoundingly, the producers had held up the start of the play. We hurried to our various seats throughout the theater. No one in the audience knew who the late-arriving crowd was. The curtain came up, and I was amazed. Unlike the first time I'd seen the play in 1964, this production of *The Sound of Music* was phenomenal, the staging of it breathtaking, and the young actors who played the von Trapp children were excellent. While making the film, we'd had the luxury of take after take, but our Broadway counterparts had to be perfect every moment they were on stage. And they were.

When the performance was over, the last strains of 'Climb Ev'ry Mountain' faded, and the cast took their bows. Then Dennis Parlato, who played Captain von Trapp, began to introduce the 'special guests' in the audience. We were scattered all over the theater, and people gasped as one by one we were introduced, for they had no idea they had been enjoying the play with the real von Trapps and the film actors.

Afterward, we all joined the actors up on stage, taking a picture with the children from the play. It seemed so natural, as if we were at a family reunion, meeting distant relatives for the first time. Nicky sidled up to me, grinning, and said, 'Here's something new. I've had a real von Trapp ask me for my autograph as well as the boy who's playing Friedrich in the play. Now, that feels rather remarkable.'

We were all giddy and I had an overwhelming sense of belonging. It was like being at a joyful celebration, not unlike a wedding. We all stood on the stage, embracing each other, not wanting to leave. *The Sound of Music* had been a part of my life for so long. I looked around me on the stage that night and realized that the circle was now complete. What had begun for me more than three decades earlier, when I slipped through the window into Maria's bedroom, was finally sanctified by meeting the von Trapps themselves, and by witnessing a new generation of fictional von Trapps giving *The Sound of Music* new life. A feeling of peace came over me. It was a perfect moment, the climax of a perfect night.

Earlier in the evening, just before leaving for the theater, we had sat on a dais at our hotel with Jamie Hammerstein (Oscar's son), as well as Mary Rodgers (Richard's daughter), Anna Crouse (widow of *Sound of Music* playwright Russel Crouse), the six von Trapps, and Dr Arno Gasteiger, the vice-governor of the State of Salzburg.

Dr Gasteiger stepped up to the podium and addressed the von Trapps. 'You have done more than you yourselves know for your country.' He told them how much their father, Georg, had helped the people of Austria after World War II with the von Trapp Family Relief Effort. 'It was Captain Georg von Trapp,' he said, 'who, on a private basis, helped the suffering Austrian civilians after World War II.' The Trapp Family Singers had collected tons of clothing and food for their former countrymen. This relief effort, he went on to say, was the largest private aid for Austria after the war. He called the six surviving members of the von Trapp family forward and awarded them each with a beautiful medallion, the highest honor bestowed by the State of Salzburg, the Golden Decoration of Honor.

Then Agathe, shy Agathe, the oldest surviving von Trapp, stood to speak on behalf of her family. 'We never expected to be honored for anything. Even our parents and our brother and sisters who went before us to their eternal reward did not expect to be honored with the Golden Decoration of Honor. But it is good to learn our homeland has not forgotten us.

'It is mostly because of *The Sound of Music* that our name actually reached every nation on earth. It created a feeling of goodwill toward us – the real von Trapps. Wherever we go we meet someone who has seen the movie. We meet these people everywhere. It is heartwarming to find such friendliness and goodwill from total strangers, and immediately a bond is formed . . . Money cannot buy such goodwill, and we owe this to the beautiful production of *The Sound of Music*.

'When we were in Salzburg last July . . . we were surprised and delighted to find that the movie *The Sound of Music*, a romanticized version of our exit from Austria in 1938, just sixty years ago, has proved to be a great blessing to the land and city of Salzburg.

'Is it not easy to see the hand of God in all this?'

Her speech surprised me, in that it focused so much on the film. I realized something as I listened to Agathe. It had always felt rather strange to receive such acclaim for playing the role of Liesl – because all I did was act in front of a camera. I'd always felt that the von Trapps were the people who deserved the accolades I received. Yet, as Agathe spoke, for the first time I saw how the film had been a vehicle for their story, and that, without it, all those who've been touched by the story would never have even heard of the von Trapps. They would never have been inspired by their courage. When the Mozart Medal was later placed around my neck, I felt it symbolized the contributions of all who had made the film and the musical possible.

Then the von Trapps stood up again. It was a surprise, unexpected. For the first time in forty years, since some in the family had left the Vermont homestead to do missionary work in far corners of the world, the six of them were going to sing together as a family. I had never even heard a recording of them. They smiled at the seven of us, then focused intensely on each other. And they began to sing. It was 'Silent Night' in German.

Stille Nacht, helige Nacht . . .

Music has been a part of my life for as long as I can remember, but I had never heard voices such as theirs, voices that supported each other, that matched and entwined so beautifully. There was something godlike in their combined voices, their intricate harmonies. They sang the first verse in German, then invited us to join them, this time in English.

Silent night, holy night,
All is calm, all is bright.

Everyone was singing, as if we were sitting in a

living room at Christmas having a family sing-along. As we came to the next verse, the von Trapps began humming, encouraging us to do likewise, softer and softer, until I felt as if I were being held and rocked, gently, back and forth. When it was over, we were mesmerized. But the Trapp Family Singers were not done. Not yet.

'We have one more song we want to sing,' said Johannes. 'It is a song we have never sung in public, but which the public associates with us – and with Austria – even though it was written in New York in 1959 for a Broadway play.'

And they began to sing 'Edelweiss.' I glanced over at Duane. Duane, who had always resisted being Kurt, who had resisted being a 'von Trapp,' or even an actor, now sat with his eyes closed, fervently mouthing the words of the song with the real family.

Blossom of snow, may you bloom and grow,
Bloom and grow forever,
Edelweiss, edelweiss,
Bless my homeland forever.

To hear them sing this song, all these years after we made the film, brought me to tears. I was shocked at the depth of my feelings as I stood alongside Nicky and Heather and Duane and Angela and Debbie and Kym singing the last lines of 'Edelweiss.' The audience in the room, now on its feet, joined with us, and the moment was eerily similar to thirty-five years earlier, when we sang it to an audience of Austrian extras on a freezing night in Salzburg. If any notes from a sheet of music can embrace a group of people, in that moment 'Edelweiss' did. All our voices built in song and in emotion, until the walls of the room vibrated.

The applause was deafening when they were done. Maria von Trapp turned around to face the seven of us. Beaming, she clasped our hands in hers and said, 'Now you are family.'

*T*he 3,158-seat Capitol Theater in Cardiff, Wales, set a record of having shown a single film, The Sound of Music, *for twenty consecutive months. When the theater finally ended the film's run in November of 1966, Myra Franklin, the widow I met who went to the film at least once every day, had seen it 940 times. Ultimately she would be listed in* The Guinness Book of World Records *for having seen* The Sound of Music *on the big screen more times than any other person in history.*

I guess that makes her one of the happiest people on earth.

EPILOGUE

Over the years, so many people have shared their stories with me. I always listen. I sense their need to tell me – to tell 'Liesl' – how *The Sound of Music* has touched their lives. Each story affects me and reminds me how truly fortunate I am to have played a small part in telling the von Trapps' story on screen.

A woman recently told me this story. She and her mother had traveled to Salzburg and, while there, went on the *Sound of Music* tour. The daughter remembers, 'I was in my late teens, and there was a growing gulf between my mother and me. But as we visited the locations where the movie was filmed, with the sound track playing inside this VW tour bus, something happened. I can't really describe it. Amid the beauty of the Alps, listening to this incredible music, we forged a new bond. At the end of the day, we were transformed.'

Many years later, when her mother was dying of cancer, the daughter crawled onto her hospital bed, trying to comfort her, asking her mother questions to try to get her mind off the pain. And one question was, 'Mom, what's your favorite memory?'

Her mother thought for a moment and then said, 'When we went on that *Sound of Music* tour in Salzburg.'

The daughter was shocked. 'That? Really?'

The mother nodded. 'The film always affected me. It spoke so beautifully of life, of family. When we were there, it was as if we became a part of that story. It was magical.' And the daughter nodded, remembering.

The mother died a few days later, at the age of sixty-six. 'She lived a full life, with many friends and wonderful memories,' the daughter told me. 'Yet, looking back on her entire life, those moments in Salzburg were the most poignant to her. Think of what that means.'

I do. I think about it often, and I am humbled.

ACKNOWLEDGMENTS

So many people helped make this book possible. I have to begin by thanking Jon Strauss for introducing Jean to me. Not only is Jean my coauthor, she is also my friend in the truest sense. I treasure her. And I'm so grateful to her sons, Tiff and Jonathan, for sharing their mom with me.

My eternal gratitude to Caroline White, our editor at Viking, whose passion and faith have been inspiring, and who has worked so hard to make our book the best it can be. My thanks as well to Barbara Grossman for saying 'yes,' and to Ivan Held, Carolyn Coleburn, Breene Farrington, and all the others at Viking Penguin who contributed to the book. To our agent, Lynn Franklin, and her assistant, Ian Graham, who believed in this book from day one: my appreciation for their enthusiasm about this project.

My heartfelt thanks to Bob Wise, Betty Levin Chaplin, and Ernie Lehman for their time and love; to Christopher Plummer for his encouragement, support, and wonderful sense of humor; to Dee Dee Wood for her fond memories; to Dan Truhitte for his help, and for singing and dancing so well as Rolf; and, of course, to my second family, the other 'children' from the film: my close friend and sometimes 'employer' Heather, and

Angela, Duane, Debbie, and Kym – what fun it's been to see them over the years! And thanks are not enough for Nicky. He has encouraged me, inspired me, and loved me. His contribution to *Forever Liesl* is immeasurable. He will forever be in my heart.

My deep appreciation to Ted Chapin and Bert Fink at the Rodgers & Hammerstein Organization, who have supported this project from its inception; to Tom Sherak and Rebecca Herrera at Twentieth Century Fox for all their efforts on my behalf; to Martin Uitz and Dr Arno Gasteiger of Salzburg, who made the event with the von Trapps possible, and who have done everything in their power to help with this book. And a very special thank-you to the von Trapp family – those who are still with us, and those who are not – for giving the world such a beautiful story, and for helping me in so many ways. I will always cherish our time together in New York, and look forward to our future 'family' reunions.

My thanks to 'the boys Down Under,' Tony Martin and Mick Molloy, for allowing me to share their on-the-air humor, and to Sam von Trapp, Laurie Lehman, Marty Garber, Mary Miklosey, Lee Beno, Jackie Warden, Kim Sandmann, Dr Jean King, Jennie and Abigail Loucks, Michelle and Kristen Crawford, Joe Symon, Heidi Stevens, Dick Christie, Mike Mattesino, Father Wayne Maro, Janice and Chip Hastings, Robin and Spencer Holmes, and posthumously, to Betty and Lou

Sacconaghi, for letting me share their stories. And a special thanks to Norman Sprague for his faith in me and for loving 'Liesl.'

I thank my daughter Jenny, her husband, Erik, and their daughter (my granddaughter!) Emma Claire, as well as my daughter Emily and her husband, Grant, for loving me and being my family; and Jay Brent, who was 'Mr Carr' for so many years and who loved me through it all.

My thanks to Sharon and Darleen – if I had to choose two sisters to help me on my path, I could never have chosen better ones. They have made me stronger and have always stood by me, as has Julie, the best niece an aunt could ever ask for. Thanks to my two nephews, Jeremy and Zevan, who, even though they are no longer here, continue to guide me in my life. And my sincere thanks to my father, Brian, for his support on this project, and to my late mother, Rita. Though my memories of them are at times bittersweet, they gave me many gifts. They gave me music.

I thank all my many friends, most especially: Mickey Levey, who was there at the beginning and has remained a member of my extended family through all the years; Michael Jackson, who let me share a portion of our story; and Libbie Agran – if there are angels, she is one. And thanks to all my Labradors: Wilson and Amber – and Zeke, Beau, and Molly, even though they are no longer in my yard. Unconditional love is a wonderful thing.

And last but not least, to all the fans who love *The Sound of Music* and for whom I will be forever 'Liesl': I thank you – and hope you will visit me at www.CharmianCarr.com.

PERMISSIONS